Solving Solvency:

100 Tips for Managing Insurance Capital in a Shifting Regulatory Landscape

By Matthew C. Modisett, PhD, FIA, MMA, ASA

1

First Published in Great Britain in 2013 by
FE Steps Ltd

Copyright © FE STEPS Ltd 2013
ISBN 978-0-9576814-0-8

Typeset by FE Steps Ltd, London

Printed and Bound in Budapest, Hungary

2

Table of Contents

Acknowledgements

I acknowledge that any and all errors in this book are my own.

With that said, I gratefully acknowledge the contributions of many people who made this text stronger and more accessible. The following people contributed to this book, either with ideas, editing, moral support or a combinations thereof:

Douglas Anderson, David Barnes, Marcus Bishop, Margaret Chan, Roelof Coertze, Erzsébet Farkas, Arthur Green, Patrick Kelliher, Ann Muldoon, Elsa Ng, Richard Schofield, James Sharpe, Elliot Varnell, Chen Wang

Spiral of Capital Generation

Generating capital is a goal of all insurers.

Some call their goal "enhancing shareholder value." Others call it "increasing return of capital." Others call it "freeing-up capital." Some just want to be larger, perhaps wanting to diversify their risks more.

Others might worry about the "volatility of capital," which is just another way of expressing the desire to hold onto capital already generated. Even when worrying about volatility, there is an assumption of capital growth that needs to be protected.

Some are worried about next year. Some worry about next quarter. Others worry about the long run. Some need it "right now," because they are having a solvency problem, or want to sell more.

Some focus on profits (a P&L issue), while others focus on capital per se (a balance sheet item).

All of them want to enhance capital, i.e. generate it.

But managing capital can be a daunting task. Where does one begin? This book provides a good beginning. It discusses ideas for generating capital, 100 of them in fact. You don't have to do them all, just the ones that make sense to you and your colleagues.

Surprisingly, many managers feel there is no budget for capital projects. That always makes me laugh a little bit. Capital projects invariably pay for themselves. The idea of no budget for increasing capital, to my ear, sounds like an oxymoron, something that makes no sense, something that contradicts itself.

Nonetheless, I understand the feeling. Some capital projects might be expensive with upfront costs and years until pay back. That does sound like a budgetary problem. However, if it feels like a budgetary problem, that means you have the wrong capital project.

There are other capital projects. There are quicker projects. And there are inexpensive projects. There are projects to fit every budget, every timeframe and every company strategy.

This is the first and perhaps the most important thing to understand. Capital management projects come in all sizes, timeframes and costs. The best way, perhaps the only way, to approach the problem is to find many potential projects and then order them. Do the easy ones first. Do the quick ones first. Generate some capital.

But then remember where that capital came from. Reinvest some of that generated capital into a new capital project. The first project was like priming the pump. The first project pays for the second. And the second pays for the third. And so on.

This causes a positive, reinforcing spiral of capital generation. I call it the Spiral of Capital Generation, obviously. It is the picture from the beginning of this chapter.

Tip 1: Understand the Spiral of Capital Generation.

The first project should be easy for your organization, and quick. It should be capital generative. It may not solve all of your capital needs, but it should be enough to fund the next project. Maybe hiring new people or talented people, or getting in a system, or something else.

The important steps are:

1. Find a lot of projects that you could do.
2. Order those projects, least expensive-quickest first, or at least choose the first project.
3. Implement the project.
4. Remember the capital savings and commit a portion of them to the next project.

5. Choose the next project and go back to step 3.

By the time you get to step 3, you are on the spiral.

I hope this seems as natural to you as it does to me. If you understand the Spiral of Capital Generation, then you are beginning to think as I do.

You might feel a bit overwhelmed by the first step, making the list. Well, that is what I am trying to do with this book. This book is my attempt to do the first step for you, to find a lot of potential projects that you could do.

Some of these projects may not make sense to you, or may not work for your organization. That is okay. I am trying to reach a wide audience. If you see a tip that does not seem right for whatever reason, move to the next one. People who have read this book assure me that there is something for everybody. Remember, all you need to do is find the first project to do. Then you have completed Step 2 and you are well underway to being on the spiral yourself.

So, please relax while you read this book. It is not necessary to understand all the ideas. You don't even need to understand all the aspects of any one idea. No one can understand all the aspects of an insurance company with all the technical details. Even if some ideas are outside of your experience, I am sure you will get the sense of how they might work. Then discussions with experts in those areas can fill in the details or help to make an implementation plan.

You should be choosing at least one idea that makes sense in your insurance company. And if you find more or a few, even better

Along the way, you will learn a little bit how I think. In fact, let me move on to that. The next chapter discusses how I think of insurance.

Chapter 2: Cutting my Eyeteeth on Capital Management.

Example of Financial Leverage: Real Estate

My career began the summer after my 13th birthday, after my 8th year of school.

I was on a roll, in a pre-9th year kind of way. I had just won an award across northern New Jersey, USA, for a computer program that composed music. The judges had even invented a grand prize over all categories just to give to me. This was 1975 and dial-in, time-sharing of a computer with 64K total memory was cutting edge. Winning a computer award for an 8th year student seemed a miracle, or really, really nerdy as my friends often reminded me. By the summer I had already received an invitation to the National Computer Exhibition to show my stuff, with "real" computer people. Me! They even wheeled in a piano so I could play new songs for people, since the computer only printed out the music rather than playing it. (Did I mention this was 1975?) I was feeling good. I had done something completely for myself and the world said it was great.

So, when my Uncle John sat me down to explain leverage, I was open to new ideas. "If you buy a house for $100, that you know you can sell for $110," he said, "you can make 10%." Okay, fair enough. He continued, "If you borrow $90, and put in only $10 of your own, you can double your money." Whoa! I get it. Less capital, higher returns.

"But what if I have to invest $100 and only invested $10 in the house?" I asked.

"Buy more houses," he said.

Little did I suspect that this was the start of my career. In that conversation, I learned one of the ways you can increase earnings on your capital: requiring less capital. I would later learn that this is the difference between return on assets and return on capital, and a lot of fancier stuff, but the basics I got from my Uncle John.

My actual career, complete with job and money, came much later. When I had learned about leverage from my uncle, my first actuarial exam was still 4 years off. I took that exam 3 months before going to college at the recommendation of my calculus teacher. I do not remember learning at that time what an actuary was. My teacher just told me to take it "and have fun." My first paid actuarial job was 13 years after the leverage lecture. Nonetheless, that conversation was the root of my career.

Uncle John never got around to telling me how you to invest in real estate. I was only 13 after all. Still, the basic message stayed with me. Managing your capital position and borrowing are the key concepts.

Years later I learned that the other way to earn more on capital is to get higher yielding assets.

By the way, that is really his name, John Carpenter, my mother's brother. His is one of the few real names in this book.

Early ideas stay with you, I suppose. To this day, I consider insurance companies to be leveraged institutions. Leverage is when you borrow at a lower rate to invest at a higher rate. This notion of insurance as a leverage strategy is not a widespread concept, but I have accepted this model for insurers for myself. Accounting leverage is the ratio of liabilities to owner's equity. (Some people use the assets rather than liabilities.) A typical insurer will have accounting leverage between 10 and 20. This represents a fair amount of leverage in anybody's book, right up there with banks.

The odd thing is that insurance companies are leveraged without using debt, per se. You do not look at an insurance company's balance sheet and see debt. You see liabilities. Conceptually, those liabilities are the debt. Insurance companies borrow through premiums and repay through insurance benefits. The implied rate of return of premium versus benefits should be lower than the investment rate. In this way you make a spread on the business. If the liability was not providing extra profit to the equity capital, why bother? If you are a share company, the shareholders want a return higher than can be provided by financial assets alone. A mutual company as well has reasons to add to the equity base: growth of the business, paying bonuses, developing further buffers versus adverse experience, to name a few.

This leverage / spread interpretation is more natural for annuity writers. They actively compare the implied return on liabilities to potential asset yields. This idea applies to more than just annuities, however. General insurers speak of an underwriting profit, essentially a spread. Unit-linked products have asset charges, which is the spread earned from assets under management. This is why insurers wish to increase assets under management, to get their spread on a larger asset base. Unit-linked products are like highly leveraged borrowing[1], where the asset-liability matching is built into the product. The block of business is matched automatically. The only risk in a unit-linked business is that either the value of the fund decreases considerably which lowers the value on which you can charge your fees, or that the customers leave. All the spread for asset charges pays extra profits to the company owner. This provides the owner's payoff for going to the trouble to collect the assets and service the customers.

Once you see that all insurance and fund management products can be considered as clever leveraging operations, the concept for increasing returns on owner's equity becomes clear.

Tip 2: There are three ways to increase return on capital:
1. **Increase leverage or**
2. **Increase return on assets, or**
3. **Increase margin on liabilities.**

If we increase the leverage by lowering the required capital while keeping the profits from liabilities the same, then the return on capital goes up. This was the lesson from Uncle John. Alternatively, increasing your asset return will increase the return on capital. Lastly you could reduce the implied rate you pay to policyholders, through managing the business in some way.

I view all capital management goals as fitting into one of these categories. For example, many speak or "reducing risk" on capital which means to reduce the variability of capital over time. I view this as a form of capital reduction. You see, if capital was highly volatile, varying a lot from period to period, then a company would have to hold more capital to make sure that there would be enough at any particular time. The volatility of capital requires us to hold that much more of it. By lowering the volatility, we reduce the need for capital, or at least reduce the amount we need. Lowering volatility allows us to have higher leverage. It also makes our natural growth rate more secure. This brings me to my next tip.

Tip 3: Realise that efforts to reduce risk are efforts to reduce capital requirements.

If we had unlimited capital, we would not worry about reducing risk. Since capital is limited, we are concerned with risk.

The Rub and the Promised Land

The trouble has been that it is not that easy to lower capital requirements. Regulators have specific rules, often with minimum capital amounts. Historically, lowering the required capital could be done to some extent, but no further than a specific level.

The regulatory environment caused by Solvency II has created the ideal environment for capital managers. Solvency II has rewritten the rules for capital management. Whether or not Solvency II ever gets implemented, or implemented in any form currently envisioned, Solvency II has changed the world, at least the insurance world. Well, at least the insurance world in Europe. The ideas in Solvency II are being implemented even though Solvency II has been delayed. The regulators in the UK allow insurance companies to adopt Solvency II models now, 2013, years before the earliest projected, formal implementation date of Solvency II, 2016. Other country regulators will no doubt do the same. The lessons learned and visions set out by the recent regulations in Solvency II, even though formally delayed, have changed the regulatory landscape. It is like a cultural movement.

For one thing, we now have a common language for talking about risk. There is a Standard Formula in Solvency II for required capital. If an insurer wishes, they can make an Internal Model specific to their own company. The most common type of alternate model is a Monte Carlo (stochastic) simulation. Now to discuss a capital model for a company, we can say, "it is like the Standard Formula, but..." and people will know what that means. Or we could say, "It is a Monte Carlo simulation with...." and people will get a barebones understanding of the model from which to hear the specific differences and nuances of a particular implementation.

More importantly, this new regulatory environment means that now we can manage capital like never before. Lots of capital can be generated over the next few years. Manage your risks well enough and you could have a zero-capital requirement. Okay, perhaps not literally. However, unprecedented low capital requirements are on offer. All those lower capital requirements mean higher returns for capital invested. Uncle John would move to Europe and go into insurance if he were not retired.

If you are new to Solvency II, that is okay. A quick read through Appendix 1 should familiarize the high-level issues associated with Solvency II. You might also peak into the beginning of Appendix 2, up to the discussion of the Standard Formula.

Tip 4: Focus on how to generate capital in the new regulatory regime caused by Solvency II.

My belief is the following:

> If you want more free (insurance) capital, the new regime is great news.[2]

For example, a recent clarification indicates that estimates of future profit count as Tier 1 assets towards capital requirements. This means profits in the future count as money today. They are as good as cash. Okay, you need to discount them and hedge them (see Tip 20) and a few other things. Nonetheless, this is a large and new regulatory benefit.[3] This is like Uncle John convincing the bank that the house priced at 100 is worth 110 and so the bank gives him a loan of 110.

You might be thinking that high mortgage loan amounts do not provide an ideal example for us to emulate given the current state of the banking industry. You would have a point, if you were thinking that. The banking crisis illustrates very well what happens when an industry does not properly understand risks. Whether you believe some bankers were willingly overlooking risks in order to reap short-term gains, or whether you believe the risks were misunderstood, one thing is clear: financial professionals, insurers and bankers alike, must understand and manage their risks.

I would like to emphasize that his book is not about skimping on capital and "getting away" with less regulatory capital than is actually needed economically. The methods here incorporate the best risk management standards. All the tips (except possibly one, Tip 11) focus on either understanding risk better or on managing it to be lower or on raising asset returns. A result of this prudent management is lower capital requirements under the new Solvency II regime.

Tip 5: Lean is not Light.

By this I mean that reducing capital requirements is not skimping on capital. By reducing risk, capital requirements come down. This is a good thing. By aiming to reduce capital requirements, we are aiming to reduce risk. This is laudable. We live in a Solvency II era, even though we do not live under the Solvency II regulations, at least not as yet. In the Solvency II era, in which we live, we get a benefit in the regulations for reducing risk. The benefit is reduced capital requirements. This generates free capital.

To do this, the general process is:

1. Identify your risks.
2. Manage your risks to lower your risk.
3. Take the credit for having less risk. (Lower your capital requirement.)

In theory, we could get to a point where we do not need to raise capital for an insurer. Raising capital might eventually be considered "old fashioned." A well-managed block of business, documented well so the regulator can understand how well it was designed and how well it is run, generates its own capital. That ideal might be harder for some product lines, but the potential is there. Even today, for example, many term-life insurance blocks are understood to be profit generating, requiring no economic capital.

So as not to get too focused on one method, I emphasize:

Tip 6 There is more to capital generation than lowering capital requirements.

You must also increase profits. This has a double effect. On the one hand, your company grows over time. On the other hand, you may well be able to take that profit (or the resent value of it) as a gain, *today*.

Tip 20 discusses VIF (Value of In-force), which is essentially the present value of future profits. This can count as capital in Solvency II. In the current regulations, pre-Solvency II but influenced by Solvency II, there are similar possibilities for including (the present value of) future profits in today's balance sheet.

Just to be clear, this is a contentious issue that is still being debated. And the Solvency II rules may well be different than the IFRS rules. In the profession, the issue is referred to as Time-Zero profits, or day-1 profits.

Whether or not you can take the benefit immediately today, increasing profits is a strong method for generating capital. It is not instant gratification, but one that can build steadily.

There are two ways to increase profits, of course. One is to increase returns on assets. The other is to decrease the implied return on benefits paid to policyholders. This book tries to explore both.

How to understand the new Solvency II environment?

If you currently do Solvency II models or want to do them, you should consider that the next trend in capital modelling will undoubtedly focus on such capital generating ideas. Whether doing or wanting to do Solvency II stuff, this book is a good first start.

In the new Solvency II environment, many of the tips work well with a Standard Formula approach to capital. (Solvency II provides a Standard Formula that all companies must use, at least initially.)

Some tips in this book are applicable only if you are making an Internal Model. (The regulators allow each company to design its own model specific to its business. For the first few years, the Standard Formula would still need to be run in parallel with an Internal Model.) Whether you are new to the creation of an Internal Model, or quite well down the road to creating one, the following insights should draw a road map to help streamline things. More importantly, these tips will reduce the capital requirement in the end.

If you are just interested in the Internal Model part, feel free to jump to Appendix 1: Overlapping Data and Appendix 2: Basic Building Blocks. You will likely come back to the earlier chapters though.

It is not a requirement that decision makers of an insurer are intimately familiar with all of the details of, for example, esoteric asset classes or option pricing models. It is a requirement that they know their own business goals. Business goals motivate capital management targets. I consider this in Chapter 3 when I discuss the motivations of different players. I also explore this issue in Chapter 8 where the setting up of a team with complementary skill sets is discussed.

Are Internal Models hard?

A capital model may be "intricate" in the sense that it has many moving parts.[4] However, intricate does not mean "hard". Fitting the pieces of a puzzle together may be "intricate," but not hard.[5] This comes in
Chapter 4 where we determine the puzzle pieces that your model must have if it is to reduce capital in your organization. By the way, the required pieces are different for different companies. They depend on the company's strategy. So knowing your motivation (Chapter 3) is necessary. Ironically, it is easier to develop a model by focusing on its capital generative aspects. This is the Spiral of Capital Generation all over again. Generating capital helps fund projects to make the capital model. Generated capital also serves to motivate everyone. For one thing, it proves that you can generate capital. It may lead to bonuses. (See Tip 8.) It gives people experience with the models. (See Tip 48.) After you get started, it never stops. It just becomes a way of doing business.

If you are worried that you might have missed the boat because you are too late for regulatory approval, skip forward to the discussion following Tip 61: (Objection) We are too late for IMAP (regulatory application for an Internal Model). You are not too late. In fact, it may be the best time to start considering capital savings.

This idea of incremental savings may seem odd to some. Many capital models are designed as one big thing, a massive system that can barely be run in the timeframe of one reporting cycle. If a company uses such systems, making small adjustments and witnessing the capital savings seems difficult to imagine. I discuss these issues in Chapter 7: Do Not Use Big Models. Mega systems, the multi-million-pound systems with similar annual maintenance costs, are unwieldy and provide little management information that can be used in a timely enough fashion for decision-making. Rarely do these systems lend themselves to on-going improvement of one's capital position.

A major theme in this book is to divide and conquer. I advocate using modular models that break a big capital calculation into bite-sized pieces. (See Chapter 7.) Not only is this efficient, but it lends itself to the capital savings Spiral of Capital Generation.

Modularisation has several advantages. Speed is one. This makes for easily rerun models in the case of faulty runs, but there is a greater advantage. Quick models can be "played with" to see the effect of changing parameters and assumptions. This builds intuition for the user and leads to more ideas for capital savings. This structure permits the model to be enhanced "on the fly" and "in the trenches" by decision makers whose intuition is constantly being honed. Of course, change procedures must be controlled in a model for capital requirements. This means that our models must be that much more flexible. We must understand these models well enough to understand potential changes. We must have developed a good relationship with executives and regulators so that potential objections can be foreseen and addressed. The structure presented here serves as a model by which top managers, such as Board members, can understand the model and its limitations without being expert in a host of different specific technical fields.

It is worth emphasizing the difference between "reducing capital requirements" and "gaming the system." The former is valid and laudable. The latter is unprofessional and potentially illegal. Some participants in the insurance industry view any attempt at lowering capital requirement as cheating. They may not say it directly, but they are resistant to reducing capital as a goal. Even without such an extreme view, there is a tendency to feel capital management, i.e. lowering capital requirements, as potentially improper. For sure, if one was trying to skimp on the capital necessary to safely run an insurer, then that would be a bad thing.

This book steers away from any skimping on capital requirements. You will find no gaming here (with a caveat in Tip 11). All the methods in this book deal with identifying risks clearly, lowering the risk through some action, and then realizing the lower capital requirement. In the Solvency II world, any lowering of capital requirements must arise from risk management. Insurance executives, actuaries and a host of others must be convinced of the lower risk before agreeing to a lower capital requirement. Regulators are included in this group of people to be won over.

This book focuses on generating capital. I do this because I find that the focus on capital requirements helps the discussion of risks. In addition, generating capital is a useful business activity in itself.

How is this book laid out?

Before we can divide a model to isolate potential capital savings, we must know our goals. We should start by finding out why we want to generate capital and how we think we can. Our "why" must be strong enough to drive us. Chapter 3 identifies your goals. Why do you wish to generate capital? Do your colleagues share these reasons or have complementary ones? What will you do with generated capital?

Chapter 4 continues by determining how we can generate capital. My view is that the use of the model dictates its structure. Before designing the model, we must have a concept of how we will manage and generate capital. We must first know the eventual uses of the model before we build the model. Your organization must have strengths that would reduce risk and generate capital. You must identify these up front so that the eventual model reflects these. For this reason, potential ways of generating capital should be identified in concept early in the process of designing models and processes.

After knowing why you want to generate capital and after having concepts how to generate capital, we are not yet ready to build the models. It is first necessary to examine our beliefs about models in order to avoid incorporating prejudices. We need to have a hard look at some of the modern myths of models. As discussed in Chapter 5: "Economics and Modern Finance: Believe it or not" even the most celebrated models have flaws. This does not mean they are unusable. It only means we have to be careful about how we use them.

With this primer about models in general, we are open to understanding the uncertainty in our models in particular. I discuss this in Chapter 6. Uncertainty is enormous. In particular, parameter uncertainty looms large over all capital models. Rather than deny the uncertainty, I advocate embracing it. By placing uncertainty in the shop window as done in Chapter 6, we can save a lot of time not calculating to spurious accuracy. My belief is that currently, a large amount of time and money is spent chasing accuracy in some areas (e.g. reducing sampling error) but that this accuracy is completely overshadowed by other areas, in particular parameter uncertainty. By admitting how uncertain we are about the basic parameters of our models, we will see the uncertainty in our final capital calculations.

The enormity of the uncertainty due to parameters completely dwarfs other apparent gains in accuracy (due to sampling). Changing parameters even slightly can have enormous effects on the final capital requirement. Small fluctuations in the parameter choice can undo most of the (spurious) accuracy in other areas of the model. By admitting how large the effect of parameter uncertainty is, we see that there is no reason to get too accurate with other portions of the model. This frees up time and resources to focus on what we can achieve. That freed up effort will lead to generated capital.

With a firm grasps of the limitations of our models and the inherent uncertainty of them, we are ready in Chapter 6 to see why small modular models are best. This chapter gets the basic form of the model in place.

With that addressed, we must get the right team in place, which is the subject of Chapter **8**.

The technical aspects of creating an aggregation model may not be for everyone. For this reason, I have relegated this technical discussion to the 3 appendices. If you are interested in these more technical aspects, then you may wish to read the three appendices after you finish Chapter **8** and before you start Chapter 9.

If after these you have any hesitations remain, I try to address these in Chapter 9: Typical Concerns Anticipated.

As a bonus, Chapter 10 presents ideas for solutions that are larger than can be implemented by a single company. Some might be considered systemic solutions in which companies with similar or complementary risks pool together for some advantage. Other ideas in Chapter 10 may be implemented by a single company, but are new and less tried. They may require additional verification to be implemented.

Do you wish to generate insurance capital? Do you accept small, modular models are worth considering? If so, let us get on with it. What would you do with all the generated capital?

Chapter 3: Motivation to Generate Capital.

Motivation
Risk Management Motivation: Regulatory Stick or Capital Generation Carrot

Why do you want to generate capital?

Capital management is not a goal by itself. There are reasons behind the capital management goals, business reasons.

For sure, if you ask a capital manager, you may get responses likes:

1. Reduce volatility of capital requirements.
2. Reduce volatility of earnings.
3. Increase earnings,
4. Reduce Required Capital (Free-up capital).[6]

Indeed, most insurers would like to do all of these things. Any capital goal will likely include a variety of elements that must be balanced vis-à-vis each other. This book aims to help find some method for doing those things.

However, these are methods for managing capital. Behind these methods are other business goals, goals for which capital is merely a supporting actor, a tool for achieving those business goals.

Tip 7: Find your true business goals before setting capital goals.

You no doubt have true goals to which capital management is merely an end. Consider the following examples:

> I am a major decision maker in a small mutual or company wanting to grow assets under management by, say, 10 times over the next few years. (Feel free to substitute any factor that fits.)

> I (We) have made some acquisitions lately and early return of the capital was a portion of the strategy. My strategy is to pay back capital to shareholders in order to increase return on their (remaining) investment in our company.

> I want to acquire competitors. I have identified specific potential targets A, B and C. Not only do I want to generate capital, I would be interested in having excess capital in certain situations when I know other targets X, Y and Z would be weak and ripe for take-over.

> I want to capitalise on excess capacity in [some area such as servicing, underwriting, investments, etc.].

> I have a major project that requires financing: redesigning products and re-educating the sales force to be able to sell products without a commission from my company.

> I want to launch a major new product.

These are real business goals. Your motivation may fit into one of these, but the above list is far from exhaustive. You may have different ones. These convey a sense of urgency, as if the company may well not be successful without fulfilment of these goals. There is also the sense of some clearly defined measures that we can use to set milestones and goals, even incentives. These are strong, motivating goals. They are strategic goals. They have a long-range sweeping scope, similar to the scope that we will need to do those things required to manage capital. These types of reasons are strong purposes. They will sustain the effort and focus that is necessary to eventually make capital changes, to generate capital. The goals contain financial payoffs that will assist funding developments. Financial rewards are important.

Let us be clear on this point: though capital models need not be hard, they will require effort from the organization. They will require effort from management. Having truly motivating reasons is essential.

Compare the above reasons with the following statements.

> Weak Statement 1: We have a corporate goal to reduce risk in the company. Lower capital requirements shows we are safer, right?

> Weak Statement 2: We want to avoid an insurance crisis like there was in the banking industry. Identifying systemic risks is important.

These are laudable statements, but difficult to turn into actions. They do not motivate like the previous ones.

The first is too general with respect to the goal. It does not lend itself to urgent goal setting. Also, it is ambiguous. "Safe" might mean more sales, higher return on capital, or other things. It might also just lend itself to a fuzzy warm feeling when you go home. It is not a goal in itself. Risk setting is a tool, not a goal.

The second is too general in its scope. As part of an industry-wide goal, a milestone to avoid a banking-like crisis is laudable. However, it is hard to translate into specific actions. In particular, this particular statement, although discussing risks, is more likely to raise capital than lower it. When the motivation is "fear or risk" then more likely than not this leads to increased capital requirements. Padding of capital in response to fear of risk, rather than managing risk, is the opposite of managing capital. Manage risks. Do not fear them.

It is possible to convert these statements into definable goals that can be put into action. How can we fashion the above weak statements into usable ones?

One example comes from a US insurer with which I worked. I worked closely enough with them to feel part of the team, like permanent staff. I will call them EUSI (not their real name). In the 80's/90's, the asset guys in EUSI recognized that a life company with triple-A rating could have an average single-A rated bond portfolio. This led to the strategy of living off the spread: borrowing at the AAA rate[7] through issuing credit-like products and investing at higher rates. Remember in Chapter 1: Spiral of Capital Generation, I gave my view that all insurance companies were leverage plays.

EUSI embodied this with a defined strategy. They did the borrowing by selling GICs (Guaranteed Investment Contracts), which are essentially bonds), to pension funds, investing the proceeds at a higher average A rate, and taking the difference in rates as the profit margin. This idea motivated their entire strategy: invest in only fixed interest (unless products linked to an index were sold), practically never invest in callable bonds, and only invest in mortgage-backed securities with the greatest degree of caution and the maximum of hedging. This strategy, however, required quite a good asset-liability match. Even a small mismatch could mess up this strategy.[8]

Notice that in this situation, "safe" was not a goal by itself. There was a more practical goal of a low funding rate (GICs that were sold with AAA bond pricing) in order to develop a company-wide asset-liability management strategy. A tight match was required for the strategy, not for general reasons of lowering risk. This strategy *required* a low risk, tight matching strategy. Lowering risk was not per se the goal, rather the goals was to capture the spread between A and AAA-rated bonds.

This strategy only unravelled when a competitor started offering higher rates than EUSI. Our marketing people were annoyed, to say the least. "(Our competitor) can offer these rates. Why can't you?" was the refrain that the investment department had to endure. In fact, the competitors were offering rates higher than gross investment yields that EUSI's investment department could get on assets. Any rate EUSI offered clients would have to be lower still because of our own charges for expenses and profit. Unless we would accept writing business with a negative spread, the strategy required that the company exit that market. After analysing the situation, we concluded that the competitors offering the high rates were having cash flow difficulties, probably caused by a troubled real estate portfolio. This was only speculation, of course, but it seemed to fit all the facts. Writing GIC business at a loss for them was a more economical way to get cash flow than trying to borrow money. In a lesser-of-two-evils sort of way, the competitor was following a sound strategy, given the bad state of the cash flows situation. (Of course, how they got into this situation in the first place might require a harsher judgement.) None of this speculation over the competitor's motivations for the high offered GIC rates changed the situation for EUSI. EUSI could not write profitable business in that environment. They had go to the side-lines and wait for GIC rate mania to subside. They ceded this market until further notice. However, the clarity of the original strategy made the decision easy. The clarity meant that the strategy's time had come to an end.

It is your job to look past the stated goals to see what the company does in practice. Are the capital-management goals supporting wider corporate goals? If not, the first job is to get these goals aligned.

This has been a lead in to my next tip.

Tip 8: Know your colleagues' goals.

There are a lot of bright people in the insurance industry. That is why I like working there. I have generally found conscientious colleagues with insightful ideas of what we could do.

The only problem is that you cannot get the horse to go in every direction at once. Even laudable goals might conflict, or at least represent compromises that need to be made. A classic example is higher returns and low volatility. This is generally viewed as a trade-off that must be made. There is no right answer per se. An acceptable compromise must be *discovered* by talking with management and colleagues.

I emphasize "discovered" in the above because the optimal is not calculated. It is discussed and will arise form conversation. It is not in the numbers. It is in our hearts. That might sound a bit sappy, but it is true. The process is more like soul-searching than analysis.

To some in the industry, the process of *challenging* the motivations of colleagues may feel controversial or aggressive. I do not think of it that way. The conversation is more like discovery than anything else. By asking what his or her motivation is, I do not mean to accuse anyone of anything. Nor am I trying to force my views. But it is necessary to come to a meeting of the minds.

Perhaps a few rhetorical questions can illustrate the different views colleagues might have towards generating capital.

Do these consultants want to perfect the model, or get on to implementing it?[9]

Is that internal manager really trying to finish the project, or is he just glad to have another empire for a couple of years? (Apologies for the negative wording.)

Is that modeller or actuary really trying to find capital savings, or just keen to look "under the hood" of a few neat models?

Is that fund manager really interested in helping you generate capital, or is he focused on an asset-only target that may not be aligned with your net capital position? (See Tip 13 and Tip 20. Also, Tip 32 and the discussion leading up to it.)

Tip 9: Know your allies in generating capital. Motivate them.

I have a view that many people in insurance companies could be great allies in generating capital. However, they may not know it now.

There are many bright people in insurance companies. All of these people are potential allies: dynamic colleagues with new ideas, sparing partners that disagree, daily grinders that see what does not work. The most opinionated ones might be the best if we can coerce them into listening as well as talking.

A lot of them are quiet. I do not know why really. Perhaps the stability of most insurance companies creates a do-not-touch attitude, either purposefully or unconsciously.

How can we wake up this sleeping army?

Incentives are one way. I mean real incentives, not the *discretionary* bonus systems where your boss gives you what he feels like. That system encourages people not to talk. Incentives should be changed to encourage discussion, not dissuade it. We should tie incentives to demonstrable results. We should decouple them from a manager's opinion of results. Real incentives are not subject to any fickle decision making process. Remember, "fickle" is not for you to decide. It is for the bonus recipient to decide. The view here is that to motivate people they must not feel the system is rigged. Is your incentive system geared to producing innovation, or is it geared towards lowering the salary cost? Be honest.

Incentives are not just about giving money out. Having incentives gives people a license to talk over issues. If the company is paying for it, it must be proper to talk about. I think Richard Branson said this best[10]:

> "Managers often assume it's a question of pay. This is lazy of them. Yes, money is important. It is essential to pay people fairly for the job they do, and to share out the profits of a company's success. Throwing money at people is not the point. When people leave a good company, it is often because they do not feel good about themselves. They feel marginalized. They feel ignored. They feel under used... Their bosses don't listen to them."

The quote is interesting. Notice the off-handed comment Sir Richard makes "to share out the profits." He says it quickly, passing over it to get to the next point. It is a given for him that you must share out profits. From that base, people get involved and start having fun. Virgin has one of the highest reputations as a fun place to work. In fact, if I recall, the salaries might be lower but the incentives for improvements and the overall fun make people want to work there, and improve the place. The fun is founded on a stable principle that the company shares the profits of innovation. I agree.

Okay, what can we do in insurance? You could pay out for innovation in capital savings. Perhaps you could pay 10% of capital savings.

"WHAT!? That could be 100 million pounds!" says the big company manager incredulously. My reply is this: if you pay that much in bonuses, your company generated 1 billion pounds before paying out the bonus. Even after bonuses that you are 900 million pound to the good. With this financial reward, you get an additional, free benefit. You have a particularly happy and mobilized group of employees and advisors, not to mention loyal. They will be ready to do it again.

Maybe 10% is not the right number. The point is that some portion of generated capital is the right incentive. It focuses everyone.

Of course, this entire area is contentious. Are we only interested in regulatory savings? What counts as economic capital savings? Should we not look at the cost of capital rather than the actual capital itself? (Many methods for generating capital have an on-going cost associated with them. These are the "cost of capital" for that particular savings.) How do we count generated capital that is not a capital savings? Is it IFRS[11] profits we should look at? Is it Solvency I Pillar 1 capital, in the UK? Is it the ORSA[12] capital? Is the target the level of capital or its variability, or the level in the worst of several well-defined stress tests? Is it something else?

Let me stop you for a second. Can you answer the previous paragraph questions for your organization? Would your colleagues give the same answer? Is there a clearly defined view in your organization as to which type of capital is important in which contexts? Is there agreement about which is the target? Can you measure it? If you are unable to answer these questions, then you cannot have an organization geared to generating capital. If you do not know the goal, you will not be working towards it.

When I was discussing earlier about companies that have well-defined goals for risk, did you believe your company to be one of them? I am not just talking about a risk appetite statement. Those are important, but are usually the product that comes after looking at the true goals. They are one reflection of the goals, but not the goals themselves. Often the risk appetite statement is merely a list of constraints. Goals are not constraints. They are the thing you would like to do or improve.

Are your answers from the previous two paragraphs in conflict with each other? Did you feel that your company had a goal for generating capital, but then find yourself unable to state what measure of capital the company targets? If so, your company may be one of those without adequately supported goals. Either the goals are poorly detailed or poorly communicated. Or there may not be acknowledgement of the trade-offs between conflicting goals. Managers and employees may have a desire to generate capital but no process or clarity as to exactly what the goals are. Alternatively, the company might not have told you the details. If the goal is not clear to everyone, it cannot be realised.

Let me ask a question. My intent is to be provocative.

Do you personally get a financial incentive for generating capital?

If you answered yes, then good for you. Do others get incentives? Why should they follow you if they do not get incentives?[13] Would you do it without incentive? If so, why? If not, why should other people?

If you do not have a financial incentive, you might want to stop at this point and carefully think about Tip 7: Find your true business goals before setting capital goals. What are your real motivations? Not all life is about money, I know. However, if you do not have incentives in place for generating capital, at least one of the following is true:

1. You are not in a position to affect capital.
2. The people deciding your incentive do not see that you could affect capital.
3. The people who decide your pay are not interested in generating capital.

Taking these in order, if you are serious about wanting to affect capital, you may not yet be in a position to have an effect. Some employees are sufficiently far away from decision making about capital to (not) have a credible "demonstrable" claim on lowering capital requirements or generating capital. If this is your situation, your first step is to change it. Get to a place where you can "do some damage." Well, get to a place to do some good.

If the second is true, you are in a position to affect capital but your superiors do not view you this way, then you have to sell yourself, plain and simple. Make it clear why the current incentive scheme (whatever the specifics) are making the company poorer, rather making it richer. It may never have occurred to them. By the way, these are likely to be the same superiors that eventually need to approve incentive schemes, or at least recommend them to those who approve them. This is especially true if the company has not had such an incentive scheme before. This is highly likely. Solvency II is new. It is not reasonable to expect that the implications have materialized for everyone.

Solvency II has drastically rewritten the rules for capital management so that capital can be generated.

Let me get back to the third possible reason why you may have no incentive: your superiors may not want to generate capital. They may say they want it. They usually say they want capital. That is just the proper thing to say after all. When you look at their actions, do you see no real interest in such activities? Are capital statements just slogans? Again quoting Sir Richard's book (p17):

> "First of all, take a cold hard look at your present surroundings. Are you really going to be able to empower the people around you?"

If you are unable to get yourself incentives, what can you do for those around you?

The first step is to know exactly why you want to generate capital. Take some time to write this down. Really. Stop reading and write it down. Why are you going to generate capital?

When you are sure you know why you want to generate capital, you should consider who around you shares this motivation (truly). It takes time to see people's true motivations. Do their actions live up to their words?

Do not worry if the environment you see is not yet perfect for capital management. It will never be perfect. We will always strive to improve. If it is not currently perfect then that is a good thing: you know where to start adding value. Do not worry if your colleagues are not yet totally in tune with your ideas. This will come later. (See Chapter **8**.)

When you think you see your reasons clearly on your goals and the state of your current environment and main players' motivations, then proceed to the next chapter.

Chapter 4: Design the Model so that you can generate capital.

Tip 10: Design your model so that you can generate capital.

"Wait a minute," you might say. "Isn't that putting the cart before the horse? Shouldn't we make the model and then see where capital savings might occur?"

Remember what I said in Chapter 1: Spiral of Capital Generation. The general process is:
1. Identify your risks.
2. Manage your risks to lower your risk.
3. Take the credit for having less risk. (Lower your capital requirement.)

We must understand our risks. We must know how we are going to manage them. These are the first and second step above. Making the model is the third step. We should already know the list of risks and our general approach to managing them before a model is designed.

A prevalent view among people working in Solvency II is that you should make the model and then worry about using it. For me, that is putting the cart before the horse.

We should not design any models without knowing how we will use them. Capital models are no different. Remember, I take a holistic view to what a model is. I describe this when discussing Deathstars. A model is all processes involved to get a final answer for capital. It may have subcomponents (interest rate risk stress, longevity, catastrophe, access to policyholder information, etc.). It may include transfer processes for results from one system to the next. Most models have some major systems for valuations supported by a host of spread sheets to feed the systems or massage the data after it comes out. There may also be decision points where "expert judgement" is used. The sum total of all these is "the model."

In particular, quite a few large UK insurers, at least, are making huge systems/processes to run models that will often take an entire quarter to run. In many cases, they cannot even run the whole model in a quarter, since some process must be done pre-quarter: calibration, decision making, etc. Certain parameterizations must be done less frequently than quarterly because the model is so cumbersome to use. By the time these models are run, they will have numbers to report, but little else.

These models are so big and so cumbersome that I nickname them Deathstar systems, as in the Deathstar from Star Wars, the one that blew up.[14]

What exactly do I mean by a Deathstar system? I call any system a Deathstar if it is too large to be used or modified. Typically, they are envisioned with the best of intentions, but the implementation gets out of hand. It may have started off supporting specific decisions or actions but later grew into a monster, one that we can barely run in any timeframe. When you find a system is only being run "to get the numbers out," it is usually a Deathstar.

Some might argue that if it is run once a year, then it is "used." This brings the question, "used for what?" My point is that a Deathstar system has limited uses. A system that runs once a year cannot be used for daily management. Some might say some to the effect that "well, we have an approximation for updates to the report." In this case, it is the update that is the true management model. The thing that you run once a year is not the model, only an exercise to update some parameters.

Indicators that your system might be a Deathstar are: is it infrequently run? Has its functionality been cut back significantly during implementation? Are the links to demonstrable decisions tenuous?

A Deathstars system is an enormous effort. They eat resources, money and management time. Costs are typically numbers that run in the millions of UK pounds for an initial package, further millions for modification, and millions for hardware and run cost per year. What value is gained from this? By the time the answer comes out there is no time left to make any changes in your business. The system takes too long to run. The complexity precludes much (actually any) what-if analysis. We have no time to do exploratory runs to build intuition about our risks. It is just an answer, a number to put in the financial statement and to send to the regulator. Users assume the answer is right, but a true check would be infeasible. Even as "just a number," it is poor since it would be infeasible to validate it.[15]

By the way, notice that I talk about processes being Deathstars. It is not the case that certain vendor packages or particular theoretical methods are a Deathstar in every implementation. There are many good packages on the market. The trick is to implement them in a controlled manner. Do not let the system and the processes feeding it drive your organization. One implementation of a system could be a dream while another implementation is a Deathstar. The label "Deathstar" is specific to an implementation.

My views on this are a product of my background.

My first job was making a market-consistent value balance sheet. This was in 1988, and almost no one was doing this. I was lucky that my first management was rather enlightened. They were a pure annuity company. They had a duration matching strategy. That alone made them different. This was the early days for matching assets and liabilities in the insurance industry. Mind you, Redington's immunization theory had been out since the 1950s. It was only getting implemented decades later.

When hired, I had almost no finance background. I had taken a finance course or two in university, but that was it. I had to review what bonds were, learn what mortgage-backed securities were and what all those "bp" things were. I had passed the first actuarial test 10 years earlier, when it was just on calculus. My high school math teacher, Mr Engel[16], had said I should take the test. I do not remember learning what an actuary was at that time. Fast forward to 1988, I had a PhD in mathematics but no job. The Berlin Wall was about to come down (though we did not exactly know it then) which caused many Central and Eastern European mathematicians to flood the market for academic jobs. With decades more experience than me, they competed for the same entry level professorial positions. After preparing to be a university math professor for so long, not receiving an acceptable offer made me feel like I had been rejected by my mother. It was nice when my boss-to-be said, "Oh, a PhD in math. We want you to help us with this."

"This" was a duration-matching model. A big name investment bank had kindly provided my annuity-writing company with a binomial interest rate lattice model used to price mortgage-backed securities. This was cutting-edge technology at the time. My first project was building the liability subroutines for this, to be placed alongside the assets. This would provide a joined-up balance sheet on a market value basis. The aim of the model was that the duration match would inform the strategy of the portfolio of fixed income assets.[17]

Notice that the purpose of the model preceded its creation.

While later running the model, we puzzled over why different products had different durations. We were thinking "average time to cash flow" (MaCaulay duration) when the program was spitting out modified durations (relative change in market value). When cash flows are fixed, modified duration is simply MaCaulay duration divided by (1+r). However, when the cash flows change with interest rates, the calculation of modified duration is more involved. We eventually figured out that the duration related to the fixed rate period of the annuity, not the average time to cash flow. If the annuity was fixed for 3-years, its duration was like the duration of a 3-year asset. It did not matter that its average time to cash flow might be 20 years. "Oh, cool," I remember thinking. It was an insight. Today this is fairly well known, but at the time, it took a bit of thought.

By successive runs and playing around with the model, we learned about our business. After that, it got easy to predict the final solution via "back of the envelope" answers.

Notice that using the model built our intuition. Quick reruns were crucial to this.

In this first job, we had two different investment managers, a bond manager and a commercial mortgage manager. Both were on-board with the duration matching strategy. Both said it was hard. A typical, overall target duration was 1 to 2 for the entire portfolio, which is quite short by any standard. On the commercial mortgage side, the "time until rate fixing" applied just like on the annuity side and the strategy was developed to offer commercial mortgages with rate resets periodically.

Notice that we could convert our intuition directly into a strategy that managers could use. The managers did not need to know the model.

Though the strategy was clear, finding commercial loan borrowers willing to have rates reset every year or two was more difficult. It is not impossible to find some, but it is easier to issue mortgages with longer fixing periods. Think about it. Most commercial borrowers do not want the risk of a rate increase to affect whatever their core business is. To accommodate the loan market, our commercial loan manager tended to issue longer duration loans than the overall portfolio target. This meant that the bond portfolio's duration needed to be that much shorter to make up the difference.

Notice that the overall target could lead to individual manager targets. We could consider give and take between different targets according to the specifics of each area and the similarities between them.

Enter Swaps:

One day, an investment bank came to presents some new ideas. It was actually the same bank as had originally given us the market value model. They were only meeting with the bond departments. Well, I was there too and technically in the actuarial department. The idea was fixed-for-floating swaps. For us it was great. Managing the interest rate risk via these instruments was perfect. We had learned that the interest reset of the annuities was driving the low duration target. (Deferred annuities, at least the ones discussed here, had a credited rate that was periodically reset to market conditions. This reset feature lowers the effective duration of the liability.) It was easy to recognize that this was the solution. Separating the interest rate from the credit consideration was exactly what we needed.

Notice that our established intuition allowed us to recognize immediately a solution when we saw it.

The solution worked on the commercial mortgage side of our portfolio as well as the corporate bond side. For the commercial mortgage department head, this was not great. It was a miracle. From one day to the next, he could offer the long fixed mortgages that the borrowers wanted. We laid a fixed-for-floating swap next to it in our portfolio. The commercial mortgage rate was fixed until maturity. However, the combination of the commercial mortgage and the swap was a floating rate asset, just as required by our annuity liabilities. Everybody was happy.

Notice that the common language between the bond and commercial mortgage departments led to sharing solutions.

This idea took off. In just a few short years, it seemed all annuity writers in the industry were investing in as much commercial mortgage assets as they could. Investment banks happily swapped as much as needed. I do not want to claim that we were the first to invent it, but we did see it independently. I do not claim that we started this idea. It was an idea that's time had come. I am saying that my first employer was one of the earliest to use such ideas.

Maybe I am simply the product of my upbringing. These are the models on which I cut my professional eyeteeth. They shaped my views of modelling. My view is this:

1. Know what decisions will be made from the different portions of the model, and by whom.
2. Build models to build intuition. Understanding is the goal, not a number.
3. Models should run quickly, to allow us to "play" with the model in order to build intuition.
4. Always rewrite your model with new insights.

By the way, many companies nowadays are concerned with how they will pass Solvency II's Use Test. While the above views are not motivated by the Use Test, if a company uses them, passing the Use Test should be a walk in the park.

Most companies have now advanced along the Solvency II model-building path but cannot figure out how to pass the Use Test. Indeed, some companies have kept Business-as-Usual (BAU) operations separate from the Solvency II program, only exacerbating the situation. If the eventual people to run the model were not present in the formation of the model, it seems difficult to pass the Use Test. It seems impossible that the model will ever be able to help manage the overall level of capital. It will just give a number each quarter.

This may not be sufficient for Solvency II. If the regulatory does not see the inherent risk management process of a company, they may not accept the final resulting figures from the model. This is true for both Standard Formula and Internal Model applications.

What decisions do you wish to have made in your company that can conceptually lower capital? Let us make sure that we reflect these in the eventual model. For now, do not worry if it is not clear how to implement these in the model.

Let us see some examples of how to generate capital:

Tip 11: Pay out in dividends any Own Funds.

It is a technical quirk of Solvency II that more assets mean more capital requirements. The first way to reduce capital requirements is to dividend out any funds not needed to cover liabilities or required capital.

Why do more assets induce more capital requirements? Consider two insurers that have identical liabilities in size and type. Suppose they have the same type of assets except Company B has more assets than Company A does. Company B will have a larger capital requirement.

Solvency II uses a "whole balance sheet" approach to stresses. All assets and all liabilities are stressed. Then the change in assets and liabilities are subtracted to get the change in whole balance sheet. The change is often called "Delta-NAV" meaning "Change in Net Asset Value." The capital requirement is this Delta-NAV. In this calculation, more assets means there is more stress on the assets.

This is conceptually incorrect. I personally view this to be a technical error of Solvency II. Intuitively, the company with more assets should be safer. It makes no sense to have it penalized by higher capital requirements because it has more assets. Nonetheless, this is the case.

If the standard has used a "short fall of liabilities" rather than a simple delta-NAV approach, the results would probably be more intuitive. This is not Solvency II, though.

Given Solvency II as it is, one method to lower capital requirements is to pay out dividends for any assets not required to back assets or capital requirements.

This is a perfect example of the virtuous spiral of capital savings. Paying out excess Own Funds as a dividend lowers capital requirements. This causes more Own Funds that we can pay out. This spiral has diminishing amounts, but it is a spiral.

Rather than paying them out in dividends, we could also use some of the Own Funds for projects. It is only necessary that the Own Funds will not be in the company at the end of the year. (See Tip 79.) For example, the Own Funds could be deployed for projects to find other capital savings.

Tip 12: Include by-country diversification of equities in your model.

Diversification is a standard technique for reducing risk. In particular, UK insurers internationally diversify their equity portfolios, with a typical UK allocation of say 60%. Our Solvency II model should reflect this. What is the effect of diversification on required capital?

For example, in 1974, the UK equity market dropped approximately 50%, the worst fall for at least 100 years. The actual figure might depend on exactly which index one analyses, but I will use this figure. This was nearly 40 years ago. Any analysis using a data set before this data will contain this figure. If your data set is 50 years long, this will look like a 1-in-50 year event. With a 75-year data set, this will look like a 1-in-75 year event, and with a 100-year data set, this will look like a 1-in-100 year event.

The standard for Solvency II is to set a stress as a 1-in-200 year event.[18] Any statistical analysis including this year will have a tendency to have a stress of 50%. If you had £100 million of equity exposure, the required capital would be £50 million. Most practitioners would agree that this is high.

One way to avoid this high stress is to discredit this statistic. Can we throw out this extreme year from our analysis? I am not advocating this, just saying this is one thing that can be considered in the analysis. The second worst year (2008) had a drop of 31%. Using this would lead to a much smaller 1-in-200 stress. There are arguments for throwing out the most severe year. Some arguments are statistical. Other arguments look at the economic situation at the time.[19] Most of these, however, leave a sense of discomfort. The natural question to ask is this: If it happened recently (and 1974 is recent), what exactly is the argument that it would not happen again? How could we possibly know that? How do we know that nothing else with a similar effect might happen? Simply discrediting the worst year and throwing it out feels like weak statistics. It may well be good statistics, but then again it may not. We should keep this year in our analysis.

The above does not consider the effect of international diversification. We should include these effects. We can see that diversification provides the right answer. This is because we (UK insurers) have global portfolios. Including the effects of this must be right. It turns out that this provides a lower stress than UK-only analysis provides. For example, if your portfolio were 60% UK and 40% something else, and say the something else in 1974 went down 9% (a bad year but not as bad as the UK) then your diversified portfolio had a drop of only 34% (=60% x 50 + 40% x 9%). The analysis of the diversified portfolio results in a 1-in-200 stress that looks like 34%.[20]

This diversification benefit is real. The UK-only methodology required £50 million in capital. The above stress that includes the diversification effect would require only £34 million. We are reflecting this benefit in our model. We could expand this analysis to more than UK and other by delineating the countries in "other". We can imagine a sub-model that would recalibrate this diversification periodically without new allocations to countries.

We might even manage to this, using different allocations to lower the risk in our portfolio and in so doing to lower the capital requirement.

In some cases, we do not decide the composition of our equity funds. For example, unit-linked funds might be decided by policyholders. In such a case, we could hedge the actual country exposure to our "optimal capital exposure." We would do this outside the fund, of course, but we would still get the capital credit for it if our model is designed to change year to year according to our country allocation.

This would require having the necessary systems to see into the funds on a basis that is timely enough to do a hedge. Even though such systems might cost a bit to implement, the savings in capital provide a huge motivation. It should be easy to justify the system's requirements if we remember the capital savings that could result.

Tip 13: Only use outside fund managers that give you granular management information to lower your capital requirements.

If it works for unit funds decided by policyholders, it can also work for funds managed by an outside fund manager. If the fund manager does not provide the information well enough to allow us to take the diversification benefit or potentially to perform a hedge, maybe we need to find another fund manager.

By the way, the tip includes the possibility of bringing externally managed funds in-house to be managed.

Tip 14: Include sector-by-sector diversification of equities.

This is Tip 12 all over again, except that the diversification is across economic and financial sectors. Dividing our equity portfolio into constituent countries yielded modelling benefits. Dividing it up by another dimension should also pay benefits. By-sector analysis is how many equity portfolio managers do macro allocations. The capital modelling and asset modelling would complement each other.

Eventually, assets could be allocated with regard to the effect on the insurer's capital position rather than on assets alone. (See Tip 32.)

Tip 15: Consider out-of-the money options for hedging your equity stress.

This is kind of a technical example. Following on the previous example of a 34% 1-in-200 year equity stress, we will learn in Chapter 6 that there is uncertainty to these figures, so maybe we actually use a 38% stress for our capital calculation. We will see in a moment why this move from 34% to 38% is not eating up our capital.

With this stress for a £100m equity exposure (let us not go into too much detail here what exposure means) there is a £38m capital requirement.[21]

Now suppose a 20% out of the money put option costs 1% of notional. Investors would say this is expensive. Their view is that on £100m of notional, the costs £1m. Unless equity market drops by more than 20% this money is just lost. Or is it?

Suppose we buy a put option on £100m. The cost is £1m. However, our equity risk has changed. If the market drops 20%, we lose £20m. If the market drops 21%, our portfolio loses £21m but our option pays us £1m back. This is only a net £20m loss. If markets drop 25%, then our portfolio loses £25m but the option recovers £5m. Again, our net loss is only £20m. In all cases, our maximum loss is £20m as shown in the table below.

Market Drop	Loss on £100m Portfolio	Payout on Option 20% Out-of-the-money	Net Results
0%	£0	£0	£0
-5%	£5m	£0	£ -5m
-10%	£10m	£0	£-10m
-15%	£15m	£0	£-15m
-20%	£20m	£0	£-20m
-21%	£21m	£1m	£-20m
-25%	£25m	£5m	£-20m
-30%	£30m	£10m	£-20m
-38%	£38m	£18m	£-20m

Even though the capital stress for the equity portfolio is 38%, the maximum loss with hedges is £20m, not £38m. We have lowered the required capital by £18m from £38m to £20m. We did this by buying the option.

This is a capital savings, but it has a cost. Each year, we need to buy a new option. That would incur a new purchase cost. Just for this analysis, let us say that this is £1m per year as in the example. The cost of capital is:

Cost of Capital = £1m annual costs / Capital savings of £18m = 5.6%

That is a very good funding rate. Most insurers would find this attractive.

This is of course only an example and the actual figures and cost of capital would be different in practice. The amount might change year to year. However, even with some variations, the above is an attractive rate. There is also a potential to use longer dated options to cheapen the annual costs.[22]

The above tips Tip 12, Tip 14 and Tip 15 are three equity ideas. They are specific. At least the first two are intuitively clear that they will have a significant capital gain. The third is also clear for those with the right background. The systems requirements are straightforward. The capital savings would appear to support the mild effort necessary to implement these ideas.

We must make sure our Internal Model supports the ability to utilize the above capital savings. Only by knowing the eventual strategies we wish to use can we make sure that the model supports the capital relief.

Tip 16: Consider taking the diversification of credit risk across bond sectors.

Credit risk for most insurers in the UK ranks as the largest single-risk factor. Tip 16 is the bond credit spread equivalent of Tip 14.

With Tip 16, we ensure that we capture in our capital model any diversification already present in the bond portfolio.[23]

Tip 17: Do not worry about index proliferation (yet).

I imagine some readers are rolling their eyes. "Is he mad?"

If you are doing a large, company-wide Monte Carlo model, on the command deck of the Deathstar so to say, the increase of indices that I have proposed in the last few tips may seem suicidal. The last few points recommend having more detail of risks, with more indices. I recommend not just a single equity index, but also different ones per country, and maybe by economic sector. I suggest using not just one credit curve, but several by different economic sectors and by different rating classes. If you are working in a company having trouble with runtimes already, this flagrant increase in the number of risk factors seems far worse than impractical. The term "mad" as used above might actually be a polite version of what such a reader is thinking.

Fear not. I do have a plan. It involves using modular, mini models. If you cannot wait, turn to Chapter 7 and then Appendix 3. However, perhaps I can keep your doubts at bay with a quick example.

For example, we can perform a mini analysis on equity returns to create a single equity model appropriate for the next step. We can develop a single model "off-line" and then use it as "the equity module" in the larger system. This would not increase run times, even though we may consider 50 countries. This new single equity model would be a weighted average of all the countries in which we invest. The weights used would be calibrated to our current allocation to countries. This allocation is probably the best estimate for the allocation over the next year. This fulfils the required one-year horizon in the Solvency II regulations. Even if you were going to use a Monte Carlo model in the next step, this equity module is not a suicidal increase in the complexity of the calculation.

The effort can be quite mild, not mad. Similarly, this is true for all of Tip 12 to Tip 16.[24]

Let me return to the ideas for generating capital.

An important risk for all insurers is credit risk, the risk for holding corporate bonds.

Tip 18: Get out of or stay in corporate bonds according to whether or not the spread supports the cost of marginal new capital.

The attractiveness of corporate bonds will vary with the circumstances of any company. The right mix of corporate credits is a new element that needs to be managed on an on-going basis.

Holding corporate bonds increases the amount of required capital as compared with holding swaps or government bonds (gilts in the UK). The extra yield in doing so may or may not be enough to support the extra capital.

Many in the industry are wondering if the best course is to simply get out of corporate bonds, sell off all holdings and never buy any more. That may be extreme. In some market conditions, corporate bonds make sense, in others not.

Consider holding £100 million of 10-year BBB bond as opposed to holding the same amount and maturity in government bonds (gilts, in the UK).

Undiversified capital charge of 10-year, BBB (20%):	£20m
Capital diversification benefit (varies by company):	£8m
Increase in capital requirement for holding BBB:	£12m

The increased capital requirement for BBB causes an increased cost of capital. This must be paid for via the extra spread on the BBB bond. The required return on capital varies from company to company, and potentially from product to product. The spread on the BBB bond varies from day to day. Let me give a few examples. In the following examples, the above increased capital requirement is assessed relative to market conditions.

In the first example, the spread on the BBB bonds covers the cost of capital:

Example 1:

Spread on BBB is 200bp: Extra yield on £100m:	£2.0m
Cost of capital is 12%: Required Capital on £12m:	£1.4m
Profit (Loss) for holding BBB after capital charge	£0.6m (Good trade)

In the second example, the spread on the BBB has decreased from 200bp to 100bp, and the BBB no longer covers the cost of capital:

Example 2:

Spread on BBB is 100bp: Extra yield on £100m:	£1.0m
Cost of capital is 12%: Required capital on £12m:	£1.4m
Profit (Loss) for holding BBB after capital charge	(£0.4m) (Bad trade)

The final/3rd example uses the original spread from Example 1, 200bp. However, the cost of capital is larger. This is not a market condition, rather a management requirement. The effect is to make the BBB unjustified:

Example 3:

Spread on BBB is 200bp: Extra yield on £100m:	£2.0m
Cost of capital is 20%: Required capital on £12m:	£2.4m
Profit (Loss) for holding BBB after capital charge	(£0.4m) (Bad trade)

Whether or not to be in corporate bonds depends on the relative yields (compared with governments) at any particular time. Sometimes corporate bonds are a good deal, sometimes not. The overall answer depends on:

A. The spread of the corporate,
B. The undiversified credit charge of the bond (on a marginal basis),
C. The ratio of aggregated capital to undiversified capital, and
D. The required return on company capital.

The overall calculation should consider:

1. Increase in <u>Risk Margin</u>
   a. This is for corporate bonds relative to government investments.
   b. Risk Margin is a component of the liability calculation reflecting the present value of future dividends on capital.
   c. Increasing the Risk Margin reduces Own Funds.

2. Increase in <u>capital requirements</u> due to holding corporate bonds.

3. Effects due to <u>matching premium</u>
   a. This is a liability valuation issue, but is potentially affected by corporate holdings.

4. Specific bond market issues
   a. Cost of curve and carry, etc.

All of these elements can vary. Spreads change over time. The required return on capital varies from company to company and product to product. The aggregation to undiversified ratio may change over time.

The point of this tip is that there is no absolute statement about credits. The correct amount of corporate bonds to hold will change over time. We can easily calculate how much corporate credit to hold. (It may even be zero sometimes.)

This analysis could be modified to include Own Funds.[25]

We need to tie the portfolio allocation decision process in with the capital management process in a dynamic way. Probably the allocation will not change too quickly over time, but it is clear that the optimal mix of credits is not fixed. It changes with external market conditions and internal conditions for the company.

Conceptually, this is the proper methodology in Solvency II for deciding how much credit exposure to have in corporate bonds. Being able to monitor this would provide a huge benefit for managing capital, and ultimately generating capital.

Tip 19: Diversify out of corporate bonds by making synthetic bonds from hedged equities.

We can replicate a long fixed bond with an expected return over swap rates by hedging an equity position. The extra return is not corporate credit risk. It is equity selection risk relative to the index. This is not an equity risk. It is only the risk or selection relative to the benchmark. This risk is comparable to the credit risk of corporate bonds, but is a different risk. Thus, by using this risk, we can get a diversification benefit. (See Tip 38.)

There are technical details[26] associated with this but they are manageable by derivative transactions that are well understood.

This strategy provides similar risk-return potential as corporate bonds. Since it is not corporate bonds, however, there will be a reduction in capital by diversifying into these synthetic instruments.

Tip 20: Hedge VIF (Value of In-Force business). Count on it.

VIF as a term is a bit out-of-date. It encompasses Risk Margin (for non-unit-linked products) and Value of Asset Management Charges (for unit-linked products). I use the term VIF because most managers of capital are familiar with it. I also like that it covers both risk-bearing products and non-risk bearing products.[27]

The analysis of VIF is complicated by definition. Exact hedging requires knowing what parts of the balance sheet relate to what. VIF is one of the three components of capital.

The other two are required capital and Own Funds. VIF is an estimate of the present value of the future profits of the business. In one of the most important decisions of Solvency II, it was decided that VIF would count as Tier 1 capital, as good as cash.

There it is. An estimate of future profits is as good as cash for purposes of calculating capital requirements.

This decision has historic roots. This treatment is similar (well as worded here identical to) the MCEV (Market Consistent Embedded Value) treatment.

I just find it fun to say, "My future profits help prove my solvency today." I suppose it is not so strange. It is just like taking out a mortgage on your home, and the bank looks at my current income, speculating that my income will continue into the future. This VIF treatment for insurers is not so outrageous.

The VIF benefit is not free. Solvency II requires that you stress VIF, and this is the rub. VIF has its own capital requirements. VIF net of the capital requirement arising from these stresses[28] can vary a lot. One estimate[28] had Allianz's VIF drop by almost £10 billion from 2007 to 2008, while Aviva's VIF has dropped by over £5 billion during the same period. Ouch. That is not reliable capital. If it changes that much then it is difficult to use it as capital.

However, if we hedge it, we can reduce most of that volatility.

For example, the benefit does not exist in the Solvency I regime, which is still required from insurance companies. In a Solvency II regime, it is not easy to do this hedging, but it is worth the effort.

We are back to a systems issue. For example, some assets are managed by external experts. Usually, we have no "peek through" mechanism to see what the holdings are in those funds. We do not see exactly what to hedge. If we did, the capital generated (or made more reliable, which is the same thing) would be so enormous that it makes it worthwhile to do so. Find new fund managers willing to give the information, or cajole the current ones with the threat of finding ones who will. This could be a lot of capital generated. I mentioned this already in Tip 13.

To hedge VIF, we would need systems with relatively up-to-date information of our portfolio holdings. We do not need to rerun the entire capital model. We need to run only that portion concerning the assets to be hedged. This brings us back to the modular model theme. We need to subdivide the overall capital model into pieces small enough to support individual decisions, in this case those decision supporting VIF hedging.

By the way, if you get good at hedging VIF, you could develop a strategy to acquire companies who do not get the same benefit. You might be able to buy a fund manager or block of business for less than the capital it provides on your balance sheet, after hedging. This idea deserves to be a tip all by itself:

Tip 21: Buy companies if you can hedge their VIF well.

The above tip might provide you more free capital (Own Funds) after an acquisition than you had before.

Tip 22: Go into alternative assets, like hedge funds.

If you have a plan to go into alternative assets, the capital model should accommodate this.

To go into alternative assets, there would be a lot of initial work. Executives and regulators would have to be convinced of any benefits, and that the company understands the risks well. The fees of many alternative funds are also extraordinary and must be considered. Is this effort worth the trouble?

I predict a reshuffle of assets after Solvency II goes live. The diversification benefit alone of getting out of corporate credits might pay handsomely for some assets. A hedge fund might yield 16%. Investing in it might produce a capital reduction (for getting out of one of your bigger risk classes, like corporate bonds). The all-in effect on capital is that much greater. For example if a £10m investment yielding 16% frees up £2m capital, then it is as if you bought a 20% yielding asset. (It is yielding 1.6m per year on a net investment of £8m. This is a 20% yield. I can hear Uncle John calling.)

The ideas above have not relied on assets providing high yields. The benefit has been the reduction in risk that leads to reduced capital requirements. However, combining good yielding assets with a savings in capital requirements is even stronger. If you like the idea of new asset classes that give great yields along with a capital savings, then consider the following.

Tip 23: Hedge inflation with music royalties.

Admittedly, not a mainstream idea, this idea is not for all insurers. It could be quite powerful for the right company. Why would a company invest in such things?

Recently, yields were about 8-10%, current cash on investment for music royalties. Furthermore, the cash amount is inflation adjusted, providing an inflation hedge.[29] Lastly, music royalties go until 70 years after the artist's death, providing an almost perpetual investment.

Seasoned "catalogues" (as a portfolio of music royalties are called) can be bought with fairly stable earnings in which you are not taking the risk associated with the star-of-today, or what would be riskier, the star-of-tomorrow. You can diversify across artists and genres, so that in the end you are not taking specific risk, only the risk that people will continue to listen to music of some type and through some media.

This point is worth emphasizing. Music royalties are collected no matter what the medium of delivery is. By this, I mean that technology has changed from records, to tapes to CD, to iPods. All along, the music royalties were paid. Even though black market downloads occur, the above attractive yields have these already figured in. All of this indicates that music royalties are a strong asset class.

Music royalties have no default risk. The royalties pay a stream of returns, but it is not guaranteed or promised by anyone. The risk is not default rather the risk is associated with how much people listen to the songs for which you have a royalty.

There are some drawbacks as an asset class. They are illiquid, lacking a secondary market. Transactions do occur but they are one-off. Furthermore, before investing in music royalties, an insurer would need to develop an internal analytic team to understand this asset class and how to fit it into Solvency II calculations. This team could be as small as one person, if it is the right person.

The above indicates that music royalties are a strong asset class, but this is a book about generating capital. How do music royalties generate capital? Consider an insurer with a large exposure to inflation risk. Solvency II requires the insurer to test the effects of rising inflation on the insurer. In general, inflation could increase future expenses of the company, or increase future policyholder benefits. The present value of these increase are additions to the company's required capital.

Insurers attempt to offset this increase in capital by buying the right assets. An asset that increases in value with inflation mitigates the capital charge. The assets increase in value in exactly those scenarios where policyholder and expense liabilities are rising. The effect is to cancel out the capital charge.

One asset class that insurers use is inflation swaps. Another is inflation-linked bonds. Equities are also used, though the link to inflation is not as tight.

Each different type of asset used to hedge the inflation risk has its own specific issue that arises as a consequence. A company could invest in equities, but equities incur their own capital charge. In the case of equities, the equity capital charge may be more onerous than the inflation charge. Some companies use inflation swaps to offset the liability risk. This creates two potential issues. The swap incurs a counter-party capital charge. The swap generally has a fixed schedule and so may also become a poorer match over time, which is the second problem. Another asset class is inflation-linked bonds, in particular gilts. However, these assets are few and far between. Additionally, a corporate inflation-linked bond would increase the capital charge due to credit.

Music royalties provide another tool in the mix of methods for offsetting an inflation capital charge due to inflation-sensitive policyholders and expense liabilities. The fact that the royalties increase with inflation means that these would mitigate an inflation capital charge. The increase due to inflation does not come as regularly as the formula-driven increases in a swap or unit-linked bond. The link is tighter than equities. Royalties are usually adjusted every third year, and the process is not formula-driven. There may be some adjustments over or under an inflation index. This causes some basis risk. For a large diversified music portfolio, however, this effect should be manageable.

The classification of music royalties needs consideration. They are not rated like a bond and could be considered as unrated credits. Alternatively, their dynamics are more like real estate: periodic income (rent is like royalty payments) and valuations are done on a model basis. In a Standard Formula capital model, there could be a debate as to which asset class to use. In an Internal Model, one could make a new asset class.

Music royalties are also simply a different asset class. This provides a diversification benefit. Diversification frees-up capital. In fact, it is one of the main tools. See Tip 12, Tip 16, Tip 38 and the 3 appendices.

Music royalties are an attractive asset class that frees-up capital at the same time.

My point here is not to make a sales pitch for music royalties as an alternative asset for insurers. I do think this is an interesting idea. My point is that if you are thinking of doing this, you should make sure the capital model can handle the asset and take any credit associated with the benefits (i.e. inflation risk mitigation) associated with it.

Tip 24: Hedge longevity with pharmaceutical research companies.

Many life insurers and pension schemes worry about longevity risk. The risk of people living longer may be the biggest risk for some companies.

Some insurers use longevity swaps to hedge longevity. Despite the occasional transaction, longevity swaps do not seem to be a lasting solution to longevity. My personal view is that the occasional swaps that are done prove that the overhead has been paid for (legal structure, etc.) and still the market does not have the momentum to take off. Why should it? Longevity swaps only spread risk. They do not reduce the total longevity risk in the system. No matter how many intermediaries there might be ready to transact, there is no end buyer of longevity swaps, no natural final taker of the risk.

The thinking with this tip is that to hedge the loss associated with longevity, you need to find a counter party who gains from longevity. Another way to think of this is, "who is causing longevity?" Pharmaceutical companies engaged in research against the major causes of mortality are a natural answer.

Pharmaceuticals are the natural takers of this risk. They have already taken it by being in the business of researching cures to the cause of mortality. They are arguably causing the longevity or at least some of it.

Furthermore, they are already taking funds. All you need to do is buy their shares. No fancy swaps or negotiations are necessary. The transaction would be straight forward.

The background analysis would be more involved. You would need to do some analysis about the potential benefits that a new drug might have and how that would affect the share price of the related pharmaceuticals. We would need to compare this with the loss on the insurer's liabilities that such a new drug might cause. This would be a new analysis. In the beginning, the uncertainty would be large. Still the savings in capital requirements, even under conservative assumptions, could be large.

Of course, pharmaceutical investments will not hedge all longevity risks. Some reasons for living longer have nothing to do with pharmaceuticals: quitting smoking, better diet, better access to medical treatment, and so forth. Perhaps there are other causes of longevity, or potential longevity, in which we could invest.

Pharmaceuticals cannot completely hedge the longevity risk. It is a common misconception that the word "hedge" means "completely remove all risk." In fact, it means to "reduce" risk. You are still hedging if you reduce risk, even if you have not completely eliminated the risk. Pharmaceuticals can hedge, mitigate and reduce risk, even if not completely so.

On the other hand, pharmaceutical companies can have volatile returns. There has been no analysis to see if any long-term relationship with longevity can overcome that volatility. (More technically, it is the volatility of the basis risk between the pharmaceuticals and the index used to hedge it, but I do not want to digress.) Perhaps the relationship with longevity is too weak. After all, I would not invest in the mafia in order to reduce my longevity exposure.

Again, my point is not that pharmaceutical investment would be a potential answer for all players. My point is that if you employ, or plan to employ, such a strategy, then your capital model should accommodate the benefit that you get from that hedge.

Coming back to music royalties, I wish to emphasise that any particular new asset class may have several ways that you could use it to generate capital.

Tip 25: Use music royalties as an alternative to corporate bonds.

As mentioned earlier, the pricing of these assets is attractive. It is also a stable revenue stream. With 8% cash on investment, and with cash flows that increase with inflation, these are attractive indeed. One strategy would have us buy a large diversified music royalty portfolio and swap it in to a fixed rate with an inflation-to-fixed swap. The rate for this could be LIBOR + something big, with something big being maybe 6%. This provides a much better spread than any corporate I know of currently. This attractive pricing may persist for a number of years.

When we sell corporate bonds and go into music royalties, there would be a capital release. By spreading our current corporate exposure over two different asset classes, the aggregate capital requirement would go down. This is diversification again coming to save us capital.

As I mentioned earlier, credit is the biggest risk for many UK insurers. Diversifying this total investment amount into another asset produces a great benefit by itself. That the asset has such a great return just makes it all the more worthwhile.

This tip is different than the previous one on music royalties, Tip 23. The previous tip was focused on the inflation-adjustment of music royalties in order to reduce our inflation risk. This was the reason for the reduction in capital savings. The fact that the asset had a good yield was a bonus.

In this tip, Tip 25, the bonus comes from diversifying out of corporate bonds. The inflation link can be hedged (with some basis risk) to provide a reasonably stable revenue stream. In this tip, the capital release comes from reducing the exposure in corporate bonds and going in to an uncorrelated risk. Like before, the fact that the asset class produces a high yield is a bonus unrelated to the required capital reduction.

Tip 26: Go into renewable energy production using proven technology.

This is similar to the previous tip, in which the capital gain arises from diversifying into a different asset class. As long as the asset class has a reliable revenue stream, it should be able to be an acceptable asset.

Some venture capital companies are looking for the next innovation in energy. That is fine for them, taking risk for greater potential rewards. However, insurance companies would need to rely on proven technologies rather than taking risks on new ones.

There are proven technologies that produce energy in stable reliable amounts. These form a revenue stream comparable to a corporate bond. There is solar production of electricity. There are wind generators that produce reliable electricity. There is also anaerobic biomass that uses waste that can produce heating directly while producing electricity and gas. These have progressed to the point that these units can yield mid-single digit to mid-teen returns easily and reliably. These are attractive returns. This is bonus when considering new asset classes, even though our primary interest is the generating of capital that arises from diversifying into new asset classes.

The production is reliable. The price of the energy produce is not. Energy prices can vary considerably, sometimes tripling or halving over a course of a year or so. There are three ways to look at this.

1. This price variation could be hedged to make a stable cash flow. This would produce a close-to-corporate substitute. Given current pricing, this could lead to a long dated fixed cash flow with double digit returns. If the hedge is done with exchange traded securities, this would incur no counter-party risk (and no associated capital requirement).

2. This variable return could be left unhedged in order to make an asset that increases with inflation, or at least a component of it. This could be an attractive asset for a pension fund or any company with exposure to rising expenses.

3. Lastly, you could use this to make new products to sell, products linked to energy prices. This idea is discussed more in Tip 75: (Misc.) Develop new products that diversify into new risk factors.

Whichever reason you find renewable energy attractive, there may be incentives to sweeten the deal further. The public relations for being green would also not hurt.

Tip 27: Make your model flexible enough to accommodate what the eventual matching adjustment will be.

The discount rate for liabilities is still in debate. For annuities, the old liability spread seems to be replaced by a potential matching adjustment, but only for annuity business. Well, that was when I started writing this book. As I am going to publishing, recent discussions indicate the adjustment may apply to all business. Alternatively, the details of the criteria for employing a matching adjustment might exclude all known products. We really do not know.

The rate at which you discount your liabilities has a profound impact on reserves. The matching adjustment is a significant issue. Your model must be flexible enough to accommodate the uncertainty surrounding the outcome as European Union regulators haggle over this component.

Tip 28: Know why you are not using the Standard Formula.

While discussing with key persons in some of my contracting jobs, I asked the question, "So why are we not using the Standard Formula?" Here are some of the answers I received.

We cannot suffer the reputational risk of not having an Internal Model.

"What?" I said to myself. I could not believe what I was hearing. I was aware of the situation that this person was working in. For them, the Standard Formula would save hundreds of millions of pounds of capital in comparison to the Internal Model they were constructing. Was it really a decision by the Board to do this for reasons of reputation? Customers do not know about Internal Models. In whose eyes might we lose reputation? It is difficult for me to believe that this is a thought out economic decision from the Board. This must be just an answer to a question that a colleague used to justify his/her role in the universe.

> We want to know the true answer.

This statement was made in a Monte Carlo environment. I discuss Monte Carlo in Appendix 1: Overlapping Data and Appendix 2: Basic Building Blocks. Monte Carlo has the reputation of being super accurate. Unfortunately, that accuracy comes only after making heroic assumptions about parameters, for example, the correlations between risks and the form of the loss function. In the particular case of this response, I was aware of a host of "simplifying assumptions" being used. These simplifying assumptions made a monkey out of any statements of "true answer."

Putting the Monte Carlo hubris aside, this answer illustrates a typical mind set in which the capital model "gives an answer." As I have mentioned, the capital model should not "give the answer," rather it should provide information to help make decisions. By managing day-to-day decisions with the capital model, capital requirements will naturally go down.

Better answers are:

> We can model this risk better. This allows us to reduce our risk and take credit for our reduction of this risk.

> We can include metrics in the model related to our decisions (hedge prices, etc.) allowing the metric to be related to our decision process rather than external indices that might be unrelated to our processes.

You get the idea.

Tip 29: Know who make decisions about product allocations.

Attribution of diversified capital is an issue I discuss in Chapter 10. For now, it is enough to know that many of the formula-based approaches are doomed to failure, and may in fact invalidate the Use Test under a literal interpretation of the Use Test. It is important to know how the company's product mix is decided, and by whom. This guides the attribution process. (See Tip 71.)

The examples of this chapter provide potentials that one might want to include in a capital model. As I mentioned, I am not pushing that any particular one must be in your model. My point is rather to give the flavour of the type of pre-modelling considerations that you should think over. Generally, you should ask yourself and your organization:

1. What decisions do we make that would have a capital impact?
2. What are the areas where we really add value?
3. Who exactly pulls the trigger on each decision?

Take time to consider this before continuing. This can be quite deep thinking. What is the competitive advantage of your company? (Hint: if you answer, "We are big," then your capital requirement will also be big.) What competitive edge would you like to develop? Where in the company would these things be done? Are there outside providers who might do it better than you might?

If you start by deciding how you wish to use the model to generate capital, you will have an easy time with one task that makes many companies suffer: passing the regulatory "Use Test."[30] By starting with the use, the proof of use will be a walk in the park. That is not the real point. Lowering risk is the real point. Passing the Use Test is just a bonus.

While you are making this list of basic strategies, you should consider the following:

Tip 30: See which of your basic strategies lower Standard Formula capital requirements.

All insurers must perform an analysis of capital using the Standard Formula. Even if you make your own Internal Model, you must run the Standard Formula in parallel. The regulators say this will be "for the first few years."

If an Internal Model has big savings which are not reflected in the Standard Formula, regulators might be hesitant to let you take those savings. They may require the maximum of the two models. Of course, regulators do not say this formally. Still, they have the opportunity to make capital add-ons when the time comes.

For this reason, I suggest starting with strategies that affect the Standard Formula. Again, his is Tip 1: Understand the Spiral of Capital Generation. Gains we make with the Standard Formula motivate and fund later savings in the Internal Model. The upward spiral of capital savings continues from there.

By the way, you may have noticed that many of my tips in this chapter focus on assets. This has two reasons. One is my asset background. My career experience makes these strategies natural for me. I have been a Chief Investment officer for an insurer and have been an Asset-Liability Manager for several insurers. I have consulted to even more insurers. The potential for managing a tight asset-liability match (to lower capital) while adding extra return has been the focus of my career.

The second reason that many of my tips are asset-based is that most insurers can implement these strategies. Some liability risks are hard to reduce. I have shown some cases where liability risks can be reduced. However, in general, insurers cannot simply change their liabilities overnight. They can reinvest their assets quickly. Most insurers are sitting on many liquid assets that can be redeployed for a good strategy. This is the reason that there will be a large rearrangement of assets in the insurance sector as Solvency II comes on line. Most of the capital reduction will involve changing the asset strategies.

This chapter represents just a handful of examples for generating capital. I hoped the list served to help you remember your competitive advantages. What are your strategies for managing and generating capital? Maybe my list even gave you some new ideas.

By the way, I am always interested in new ideas for generating capital. If you think of new ones, please let me know. I always love to hear them.[31]

Chapter 5: Economics and Modern Finance: Believe it or not.

"The world's smartest man just jumped out of the plane with my backpack!"

One of my favourite jokes goes like this:

> The pilot and everyone one else have jumped out of an airplane about to crash. There are four men left but only three parachutes. As it turns out, the four men are the President of the United States, the world's smartest man, a priest and a bum. (There must have been a mix up in seat reservations.)

> The President of the USA says, "I owe it to my country to save myself." He straps on a parachute and jumps out of the plane.

Not missing a beat, the world's smartest man points a figure in the air and declares, "I owe it to the world to save myself." He straps up and jumps out of the plane.

The priest looks at the other man and says, "I am old and you are young. Save yourself with the last parachute."

To this the other laughs and replies, "Don't sweat it Padre. We're okay. The world's smartest man just jumped out with my backpack."

When Harry Markowitz retired, he allocated half his money to bonds and the other half to shares.[32] When asked why, he responded, "to minimize regret." Here is a Nobel laureate renowned for portfolio theory for allocating assets choosing his Own Funds allocation to reduce his future psychological pain when things eventually go against him. I chuckled when I read this. It seemed like the Pope had refused last rights. This is a complete turn of one's back on one's own theory after having received a good career from it. You have to smile at that, especially the candour of the statement.

Since Dr. Markowitz deviated from his own theory when the time came, and since he was good-natured enough to share the irony publicly, perhaps he would not mind that I start my discussion of misconceptions with his theory.

Tip 31: Risk ≠ Return.

I recall introducing a project for home mortgage offerings in Eastern Europe. This particular country had no mortgages at the time. It was an untapped market. The first to enter would be at a big advantage. The project would have yielded over 25% annually even with our extremely conservative assumptions. Not just my team was saying so. There were external advisors confirming our analysis. Despite all the analysis, the Board wanted to reject the plan. Their reason was that the return was too high: "There must be risk somewhere." After turning it down, a competitor adopted essentially the same plan. They made over 40% annual for the next few years until competition came and lowered the rates to more normal, but still high, returns.

Granted, some investors do not look at risk and just go for estimated return blindly. I do not advocate that. Certainly, when someone presents me with a high return opportunity, my initial reaction is to be wary. Often, if it seems too good to be true, then it is too good to be true.

However, that is not an absolute. While being cautious, we also want to be open. If the deal is bad, with a little digging, you can usually see the trick, or the tell-tale conflict of interest. It is a different matter to have a prolonged analysis of business and then relying on that analysis. After all, companies are in business to make exceptional returns. Certainly specialized knowledge in certain areas makes that possible. The catch phrase

"Risk equals Return" can blind you to possibilities. Another blinding phrase is, "more return, more risk."

Let us examine from where this came. The source was the Capital Asset Pricing Model, from Markowitz. Actually, to my knowledge he never said this in the absolutist manner that it is typically used. Markowitz never said it like the above-mentioned Board did. How does the theory go?

All investments can be assessed according to their expected return and their risk, which is usually interpreted to be the standard deviation of returns or perhaps volatility. I use modified duration as the measure of risk, for illustration. If you prefer, you can think of maturity or term. The return versus risk of all assets in our universe of possible investments can be graphed and the result looks something like the following.

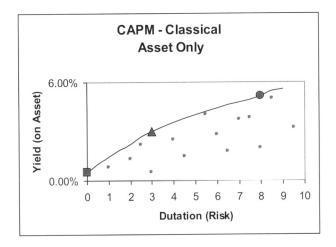

Efficient Frontier (Asset Only). The upward sloping line is the efficient frontier, a border at the top of all investment possibilities. A risk-free asset (■) representing overnight deposits with zero duration has been included. The points below the efficient frontier represent inefficient investments, less desirable investments than those on the efficient frontier.

Notice that greater risk means greater return and vice versa <u>only</u> on the efficient frontier. If we know we are along the efficient frontier, then risk equals reward. However, how do we know we are on the efficient frontier? We may not be. Many investors are not. Someone is investing in those orange dots in the graph above.

In fact, many investors stop looking for better returns or lower risks simply because they assume risk = return. They may well be below the efficient frontier, but since they assume that any increase in return must be an increase in risk, they stop checking. If they looked, they would find higher yielding investments with the same risk. They could find the same yields with lower risk. If they looked, they could improve both. But they don't look. They don't believe they need to look. The efficiency of the market will do it all for them, in their view.

CAPM does not say to stop looking. I do not believe Markowitz ever said to stop looking. The theory encourages us to look for better situations. All those points in the middle of the graph are situations in which management can make things better. Perhaps our portfolio is one of those points below the efficient frontier. How would we know? The only way to know is to look for alternatives and see if any give a higher return or lower risk. Only by checking can we know. It is not automatic that risk = return. We must work to get to the efficient frontier even if we accept the CAPM model.

Many insurers have such systems that they cannot even say what the exact composition of their portfolio is. There could be many reasons for this. It could be due to the use of external manager, antiquated internal systems, timing issues with bookings, insufficiently detailed models for structured products or private equity or real estate, or in many instances simply errors. In such bureaucratic organizations, it is difficult to assume that the portfolio is efficient.

Markowitz goes on to say that the market itself is efficient. That seems a leap of faith. Most investors worth their salt know that it is easy to beat any fixed index. A formula driven index cannot beat a modicum of thought. A formula-driven, market index that lumps the good in with the bad does not seem like an example of efficiency. It seems like a benchmark, nothing more.

While I am on the topic, it has never been clear to me that a rational investor must prefer a riskier investment.[33] The literature has covered this issue sufficiently, so we do not cover it here.

Despite general reasoning as presented above, many managers assume that if you are earning more, then you must be taking on more risk. This is simply not true like a law of nature. More return could mean more risk. It could mean that you have moved from something below the efficient frontier to something towards it.

If you have done any market consistent valuations or thinking in your career, then this point could feel uncomfortable. "How can it be that one asset consistently outperforms another? Would not market participants buy and sell to remove the 'anomaly'?" There are three answers to this question.

First, to reduce the price discrepancy via market transactions, it would be necessary to sell the dear and buy the cheap. As long as you and other market participants continue to do this, the prices would tend to get closer together: selling the dear would bid down the higher price while buying the cheap would bid up the lower price. Eventually they would meet. This is the arbitrage-free argument. Can the market continue these transactions sufficiently to cause the prices to convergence? There are only so many governmental bonds to buy and corporate bonds to sell. Eventually, exhaustion would stop the transactions. We do not have infinite capacity in our portfolios. When our capacity to transact runs out, the discrepancy would remain.

Second, the CAPM indicates that some investments are efficient and others not. Something has to be below the efficient frontier. It would seem CAPM as a theory is at odds with the idea of arbitrage-free pricing. Is it? Arbitrage-free pricing works only if the object being sold and bought are viewed as the same thing, or at least interchangeable. The arbitrage-free effect of converging to the same price breaks down when market participants view the objects differently. Converging to the same price fails to take place simply because market participants view, for example, corporate bonds and governmental bonds to be different. Said as economists would, the view (not the fact) that governmental bonds are default-free makes the demand for these assets greater (makes the yield lower).

Third, pricing "anomalies" do persist. That is to say, there are persistent differences in prices that are not anomalies and are consistent sources of extra return. We have examples of this. Insurance is an example. A basic tenet of insurance theory is that policyholders pay a premium higher than their expected benefits. This is utility theory. Avoiding the catastrophic loss make them comfortable with an expected small loss. This difference in value persists and forms the core of the viability of insurance companies. Without it, insurers could not write new business. Policyholders must consistently have a different transaction price than insurers. Otherwise, the insurance market would break down. Insurers count on this discrepancy to persist.

The investment market is the same. Some assets trade at a consistent premium or discount. For example, GMAC (General Motor Assurance Corporation) provides financing for cars. For its credit class, it consistently provides a better yield and did for years. The reason is supply and demand. There is so much of this particular credit in the market that it consistently trades at higher yields (discounted prices). If they did not offer a better yield, they would not be able to place all of these bonds. The market would be saturated. The higher yields on these bonds are not a statement about the creditworthiness of this particular company. The parent company is comparable to others of the similar rating. This effect is due to the huge supply of this paper on the market.

Some asset classes may just be better than others in a fundamental and persistent way. Could that be true? Can there simply be good deals as much as there are simply bad deals. That seems an affront to efficiency. The truth is even stranger.

Tip 32: "Efficient markets" is a nonsensical idea. Risk depends on the beholder.

Let me continue with the previous example of an efficient frontier. I want to bring asset-liability management into the picture. We manage capital, not assets. This is a main assumption of this book. The point for insurance companies is the return on capital, assets net of liabilities. How does the situation change if we consider assets net of liabilities?

Placing the two situations side by side, the following graphs illustrate how the asset-only CAPM and the asset-net-of-liability CAPM compare. I assume our liability has 3-year duration. Investing in 3-year assets removes any interest rate risk, and represents the strategy with no risk. In the Asset-Only case, there is a 3-year asset (▲) on the efficient frontier. In the Asset-net-Liability case, this becomes the risk-free position. More interestingly, the zero-duration (■) is along the efficient frontier in the asset-only case, but in the asset-net-liability case it falls off the efficient frontier.

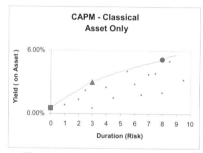 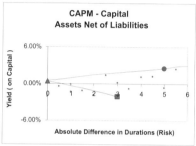

Figure: The efficient frontier changes when assets net of liabilities are considered. The two situations do not agree which assets are along the efficient frontier.

The efficient frontier changes with the liabilities of the investor. Risk depends on who the investor is and what her liabilities are. It is not inherent to an asset.

This is a simple numerical example. Its implications are profound. The first graph might be how a total return manager views the universe of investments, while the second is how an insurer (say, an annuity writer) views the universe. These two "rational" investors do not even agree about which assets are on the efficient frontier. Their view of risk is entirely dependent on their liability structure. The first had no liabilities while the second did. If we had a third investor, say with an 8-year liability, the graph would be different again.

The profound implication is that risk does not exist in the security. There is no consensus among investors over a given security's risk profile. There is no objective statement of risk about a single asset. Risk is in the eye of the beholder.

Assets are like any other tool. They are productive in some hands and dangerous in others. A hammer is useful in a carpenter's hand. It is dangerous in a serial killer's hand.

If we take this further, we can ask the question, "How do different investors compete (bid) on the various assets?" The 3-year liability player might be willing to bid up the 3-

year asset because it is his risk-minimizing strategy. Even at a higher price (lower yield), it may be attractive. That same player would shun the shorter assets since they are so unattractive. This is all rational. This lack of demand might reduce their prices (increase their yields).

To the no-liability, asset-only player these movements in yield seem irrational. This is just like the pack of cigarettes sliding across the dashboard of a turning car; if your frame of reference was only the inside of the car and you felt no momentum, as if you are watching it on film, the slide across the dashboard is mysterious. The frame of reference is important. The bidding up of 3-year assets and down of shorter assets is irrational if only viewed from the no-liability perspective.

If we ask the question, "Are markets efficient?" it is a nonsensical question. It presupposes that there is a single view of value for assets, some objective inherent worth. The question assumes that value is homogeneous amongst market participants. It assumes everyone agrees about value. Nothing could be farther from the truth. The question's inherent assumption makes us believe that the only question is whether, or to what extent, the market reflects the true value. The reality is that since value is relative, depending on your own liability structure, there is no single view of value. Opinions are mixed, heterogeneous. Since there is no single, objective value, it makes no sense to discuss whether the market reflects this value.

There is an old joke in which the newspaper reporter asks, "So, mayor, are you still beating your wife?" The mayor is stuck. If he answers "No," then he is admitting that he did beat his wife. If he answers "Yes," then he is also admitting it. The trick is in the wording of the question. It presupposes that some beating took place at some point. The word "still" is the crucial one. Some questions, by their very wording, set up the answer. The poor mayor gets roped into a conclusion no matter what he answers. Even staying silent seems to accept the beating premise.

The question, "Are markets efficient?" is equally loaded. The wording of the question gets you in the wrong mind set. It starts you wondering if, or to what extent, true market prices reflect (true, homogeneously perceived, universally accepted) value. It presupposes an absolute value, in a quite subtle way. The problem is that there is no inherent value.

The truth is that the question has a false assumption. It is nonsensical. There is no absolute objective value, no measure of risk, to make the question meaningful. Risk is not a characteristic of an asset. The risk of an asset depends on who uses it and for what purpose.

I would even go further. A market needs differences of opinion in value to function. If everyone agreed on the price, what would be the point in trading? If we were betting on a horse race but everyone was to agree on which horse would win, there would be no bets placed. It does not matter if our opinion of the winning horse is correct or not. If we all had the same view, there would be no market. Divergence of opinions is a necessary component for a functioning market. The efficient market hypothesis implicitly assumes the existence of a homogeneous opinion across market participants. In fact, market views are heterogeneous, and must be if the market is going to exist.

So Risk $\neq$ Reward. The concept of efficient markets is a vacuous concept. This false concept gets us in the wrong mind set to think about risk. Our view of risk is potentially unique to us, and our situation.

In the end, the CAPM is a useful conceptual tool. It has shown us the folly of efficient markets, and pointed out the unique requirements stemming from our own asset-liability management. This is not quite how Dr. Markowitz may have intended it. Nonetheless, this is useful.

Let us move on to another couple of Nobel Laureates.

In 1998, Long Term Capital Management lost $4.6 billion in less than four months requiring financial intervention by the Federal Reserve Bank, and the fund closed in early 2000. John Meriwether, the former vice-chairman and head of bond trading at Salomon Brothers, founded long Term Capital Management in 1994. The Board of Directors' members included Myron Scholes and Robert C. Merton, who shared the 1997 Nobel Memorial Prize in Economic Sciences. A primary contribution to economic theory from these last two individuals was the development of the Black-Scholes (Merton) pricing model for financial options.

It is good to put the Long Term Capital Management event in context. Central banks are not in the habit of bailing out hedge funds. The fact that the Fed got involved demonstrated that this particular loss was large enough and with enough connections to other institutions to potentially topple the financial system.[34] This represents a disastrous showing of financial models. Merrill Lynch, hardly a bastion of anti-capitalist sentiment, observed in its financial reports that mathematical risk models "may provide a greater sense of security than warranted; therefore, reliance on these models should be limited."[35] If ever there were a case of damning with faint praise, this is it.

It certainly feels that something is rotten in the state of Denmark. (I know the Nobel prizes come out of Sweden. My reference is to Hamlet.) One Nobel laureate does not believe in his own theory, and two others have had their theories challenged in the wake of a financial disaster. Good thing we do not use those models anymore. Oh, wait! We do.

Long Term Capital Management employed Value-at-Risk, a more general version for the 1-in-200 paradigm, the central tenant of Solvency II. The uncertainties around the estimates that led to Long Term Capital Management's downfall are written into the DNA of Solvency II.

The reliance on tail correlations is also cited as a reason for Long Term Capital Management's downfall. Solvency II relies on tail correlations as well. Long Term Capital Management and Solvency II share these models. They share the weaknesses inherent in these models. Are we setting ourselves up for a systemic disaster?

Perhaps we should not judge these theories according to the experience of one company. After all, the models employed by Long Term Capital Management were not used on an industry-wide basis. To my knowledge, they were not blessed by academic rigour. There were no articles that went through peer review in a journal.

However, we can look at a theory that has passed such review, one that is used by a whole industry. The market employs Black-Scholes-Merton option pricing model today. More to the point, insurance companies employ this model's principles when building their systems. How does this theory fare under scrutiny? Perhaps you saw the next tip coming.

Tip 33: Black-Scholes option pricing theory is wrong (but still useful).

If this is news for you, I can sympathize. It was surprising for me when I heard it. Believe it or not, there is something called the volatility smile, a known "issue" in modern finance[36] which demonstrate the assumption of the Black-Scholes options pricing model to be false. The theory supporting this model, widely used the world over, is wrong. It is not modelling the universe, or even markets. Furthermore, this is a known "issue," an accepted issue in modern finance. This is not just me saying so.

This is not a problem in my view. Perhaps this surprises you. We still use the Black-Scholes option-pricing model, even though it is wrong. I am okay with that. Why do we do this? The answer is that Black-Scholes is only a pricing convention. It is only a convention for making sense out of many different prices. It does not have to be right, like a physical law. It just has to be convenient.

In this sense, it is like Internal Rate of Return (IRR). Any elementary text on finance, when introducing IRR mentions some drawbacks with it as a measure: IRR assumes all interim cash flows are reinvested at the IRR rate. Also projects of different duration are not entirely comparable; streams of positive and negative cash flows might have multiple possible values of IRR. Nonetheless, practitioners routinely use IRR even if they know its limitations. After all, it is just one measure to help us understand a project or to compare disparate prices. IRR is not an economic analysis of future yields. In fact, when we calculate forward rates from current yields, we routinely dismiss them as unreliable predictors of the future. We know the limitations of this measure. For that reason, we can use it.

Similarly, implied volatility is just a measure to help understand option prices. It does not predict the future of volatility of securities nor price securities. It is a convenient pricing convention. We would not use it as the only basis for buying an option.

Most pricing "models" are actually fitting exercises. Enough variables are introduced to be able to fit any prices that occur. As long as the parameters have at least a modicum of theoretical justification, market participants use them and feel they are adding value. As long as these new parameters change the final price significantly, enough to accommodate prices observed in the market no matter how wild, then the better the parameter can be accepted.

Bizarrely, this is the opposite of what most scientific professions would like. Those professions would like a final answer to be as insensitive to the measured parameters as possible, so that any error in measurement would not lead to invalidation of the final use. For example, if an engineer was making a bridge, she would like to know that the alloys used with those suspension wires and pylons and so forth, lead to a structure that can bear a load of X, to within a good margin of error. She would test the structure's breaking point. The breaking point estimate should be reliable and accurate. This allows her to design the bridge in a way to avoid that breaking point. Suppose on the other hand, her bridge model allowed for a volatility-like parameter. With this sensitive parameter any test of the breaking of the bridge could be justified by varying the volatility parameter. She could adjust the volatility parameter to explain any particular breaking point: bridge broke at 1 million tons, then volatility is A; broke at 16 ounces, then volatility is B, and so forth. Such a model would be completely unacceptable to the engineer since it would be useless in the quest to make a stable bridge. If we can adjust the model to accommodate any tested breaking point, we are essentially saying that we cannot predict the breaking point.

Why do I go on about this? Partly I am expressing a general caveat about not relying too much on models. In this particular instance, do not rely too heavily on models simply because they match prices. If a modeller adds enough parameters, he can match any data. This does not mean it models reality. It only means more free parameters provides a tighter fit. This is cheating. Adding enough parameters always gets a better fit. Adding parameters may not increase our understanding.

However, there is a more general reason for my discussing this particular limitation of financial modelling. The above comparison with the engineer shows how predictive models should not have loose variables that explain anything. Are finance models predictive models? Not really. In many applications, the financial variables are not predicting anything. IRR does not predict future interest rates. Implied volatility does not predict future actual volatility. It does not predict possible levels of prices. These tools serve a different function: they allow comparison of different options. Given two projects, the one with the greater IRR seems at first look the better bet. Of course, IRR as a tool has flaws, so it is only one thing we would look at when comparing projects. Expected cash flow, uncertainty over cash flows, and the ability to undo a transaction (liquidity) are all examples of other considerations. The models have a prediction of each project in the future (like the cash flows on a bond), but not on the IRR itself.

Similarly, implied volatility can be used to compare two securities to speak of the relative riskiness (inherent in the pricing). Of course, all the shortcomings of volatility have to be understood to use it as a tool; for example, you cannot easily compare volatilities of securities (options) with different strike levels. This drawback (the volatility smile) does not render the implied volatility useless. It still has a great many uses, in asset-liability matching, for example, where liability and asset models arguably have the drawback cancel out as long as the same model is used for both assets and liabilities.

The above discussion supports the next tip.

Tip 34: Asset-Liability Management models compare fruit to fruit, though they may not be apples.

We use asset-liability management models to offset risks against each other. This is done without absolutely valuing the risks involved.

An old adage of asset-liability managers is, "You must use the same model for assets and liabilities." Consistency of the asset model and the liability model is more important than any particular nuance of the models. What would happen if we use a single scenario liability model in conjunction with a stochastic asset model? Absent any reasoning that these models were comparable, or identical in this certain situation, we would be unable to make meaningful comparisons. It would be apples versus oranges. Most asset-liability managers understand this intuitively. It is so natural to them that they may not even recognize it as a principle of asset-liability management. It simply is true.

We must not compare apples to oranges. We must compare the same fruit. With asset-liability management, it is not important if it is apples to apples, or if it is oranges to oranges, or cherry to cherry for that matter. It just has to be the same fruit.

The next step however is to realize that asset-liability management's claim to fame does not depend on any absolute valuation, only the difference between valuations. For example, assume you own a share and you sell a forward[37] against it, looking in the future price of the two positions netted together at the forward price of the future. We know the net difference of these two positions. It should be a fixed return. Though we know the net of the two positions, we may not know the actual value of either. We cannot predict the value of the share at expiration, but we can hedge it. This is the essence of a lot of asset-liability management. We know something about the difference of two prices. We may not be able to say much about a single price.

What would happen if we used different pricing models for the forward and the share? For example, the forward might be calculated as discounted projected price minus current market price, while the share was valued via a dividend-discounted model. The differences arc likely to be meaningless. More importantly, it would be useless.

Tip 35: You need more than Asset-Liability Management models to calculate capital.

Do not let the success of asset-liability management fool you into thinking that you need only those models to set the level of capital. You need something more.

The reputation of asset-liability models is quite strong, rightfully so. These models calculate the difference between assets and liabilities well. However, this does not mean these models know the individual values of assets or of liabilities. [38]

Said in a geeky way, asset-liability management methods excel at calculating sensitivities (say to interest rates) without necessarily placing an absolute price on cash flows. For example, consider doing a duration match on a stream of annuity liabilities. Whether you use government rates, swap rates or a corporate-laden rate for discounting, the durations tend to be fairly close to each other. These differences would not affect a duration matching strategy in any significant manner. The asset-liability management process is reasonably insensitive to this choice.

On the other hand, if liabilities were valued at risk free rate (either governments or swaps) but bonds were priced with a corporate-laden rate (either full spread, or one reduced for defaults) the present value difference would be enormous. This in fact is a major theme in Solvency II, getting the discount rate for liabilities correct: formerly known as the liability spread, now known as the matching adjustment.

Tip 36: There is no risk-free rate (or more than one).

In "This Time is Different: A Panoramic View of Eight Centuries of Financial Crises," Carmen Reinhart and Kenneth Rogoff examine data extending back to 1800 covering more than 90% of the global GDP. They note that there are "long periods where a high percentage of all countries are in a state of default or restructuring. ... serial default on external debt – that is, repeated sovereign default – is the norm throughout every region in the world, even including Asia and Europe." They offer a lucid account of default, providing evidence that, even on domestic debt, countries may choose to default rather than allow hyperinflation. The rates of defaults, emphasizing the large coverage of world sovereign debts, regularly is over 10% with long periods over 20% and even extended times over 30%. In the face of this evidence, it seems difficult to claim that any of these countries debts represent a risk-free rate.

The authors discuss countries that may have graduated "from the perennial problem of serial default." This would seem a departure from the main theme of the paper: that countries have significant probabilities of default. The graduated countries seem to be England, Greece, Spain, Austria, Germany and possibly Chile and Mexico. Even while stating this, they pull back from the conclusion that these countries have graduated by saying, "If history tells us anything, it is that we cannot jump to 'this time is different' conclusions." The authors have hedged their conclusions about graduation away from serial defaults. I emphasize that even their wording "from the perennial problem of *serial* defaults" (emphasis added) only serves to stress that all countries have some probability of default.

Certainly, the crisis in the PIIGS (Portugal, Ireland, Italy, Greece and Spain) makes the inclusion of Greece and Spain particularly unsupportable. I do not claim that any of these countries will default. I do claim that their chance of default is higher than zero.

Even if we wanted optimistically to press the case for graduation to a special class of countries that have no chance of default (a stronger proposition than Reinhart and Rogoff toy with) the evidence is against us. The best we could say is that some countries have not defaulted recently. That is much weaker than a zero percent chance of default. Given the number of countries in the study (90% of the world by GDP), simple random chance would have some not having defaulted recently. That does not show zero chance of default. The laws of statistics indicate that some would have that record, perhaps for no special reason other than luck.

Reinhart and Rogoff also mention "default virgins" such as the United States, Canada, Australia, New Zealand, Norway, Sweden, Finland, Denmark, Belgium, Hong Kong, Malaysia, Singapore, Taiwan, Mauritius, Thailand and Korea. The last two countries received massive IMF loan packages in the late 1990s to avoid default, but still count as default virgins. It is an interesting list since it ignores some technical defaults (such as the United States lowering its currency's gold content). Given the short span of political independence of many of these countries, the thesis still seems difficult to conclude that the probably of default is zero.

Just because someone is a virgin today, does not mean (s)he will always be. The chance of losing virginity is greater than zero.

Why do we speak of a risk-free rate?[39]

My answer is that this is the pricing convention. We do not really believe there is a zero chance of default. It just makes our models neater if we use zero-default as a pricing convention.

We could argue that this assumption is deluded. We could argue that this assumption conflicts with the past (as the above authors support). We do not need to. The risk-free assumption is a convenient pricing convention. It negates any need to muck up our models with estimates of defaults for the countries. This is sufficient reason to use this assumption. By the way, this assumption is changing in practice. There is a move away from the assumption that all sovereign bonds are default free. In particular, in Europe, there is a differentiation being made between countries. The feeling now is that there is one base risk-free rate, and some countries' debts are price higher yields and the potential of default must be considered.

Consider the chaos that might ensue if we did not use a risk-free assumption. If our models had default rates for countries, there would be different opinions about the default rates of the countries. Yield calculations would have to have caveats regarding the default assumptions. The situation would be complicated, but add little value. Imagine the havoc such government-default considerations would cause to corporate bond models. We often use a government rate as a base over which you add a corporate spread. Messing up the current pricing conventions by adding a governmental default rate into the parameters would complicate things. What would be the value? It is better just to leave it out. Assume no default in the pricing convention. We can handle any concerns of governmental default outside of the pricing model. Just as before with IRR, since all the market participants know the limitations of the risk-free assumption, it is easy to use a zero-default assumption in pricing. We consider default possibilities separately.

The danger is that perhaps some people begin to believe the zero-default probability. Indeed, since Black-Scholes uses of the risk-free rate the last few decades have seen the concept become a type of mantra.[40] However, when a country starts having serious problems, we pull it out of the pack, give it a new label (like PIIGS) and start examining the greater-than-zero-default-probability implications in earnest.

Wait a minute. Tip 36 said there might be more than one risk-free rate. If there is no such thing as a risk-free rate, how can there be more than one? What is that all about?

A diversified portfolio of bonds can provide a "risk-free" yield that is higher than government yields. With the lessons learned above, that the supposed risk-free rate associated with governments is a misnomer and there actually is some risk there, what does this mean about corporate bonds? In general, corporate bond spreads (over government) are greater than even the most conservative estimate of defaults. Perhaps not all bonds, but generally for investment grade bonds. Thus, a well-diversified bond portfolio should be able to achieve any excess return over governments, after defaults, which is significantly positive.[41]

At this point, the true believers of risk-free rates jump on the probabilistic wording of the last sentence. They accuse the highly probable excess corporate spread of being "Not perfectly risk free." The argument continues that the taking of risk, no matter how small, with perhaps some utility theory words leavened in for good measure, makes the comparison of the diversified excess corporate spread to be incomparable with the true risk-free rate of government bonds. No matter how diversified (how large n is, if you read the endnote), the comparison of the excess corporate spread to governmental yields is apples and oranges.

However, with what we have seen, governmental rates are not risk-free. They have default probabilities. Is the above-mentioned diversified, excess corporate spread incomparable to the governmental yield? You have probably figured out the direction in which I am heading.

The excess yield from a diversified corporate bond portfolio has a probability of default. This is comparable to the actual possibility of default on government bonds. Neither of these is so special as to deserve the title risk-free. Both governmental bonds and diversified corporate bonds portfolios have a chance of default.

Which investment is a better deal? This depends on the analysis you do. You may think the government bonds have less chance of default, but this just might be a residual effect of the risk-free brain washing. The evidence is that there are quite large chances of governmental defaults. There are many more corporate bonds than governmental ones, providing a greater chance of diversity. This is an advantage for corporate bonds.

The devil is in the details: what are the actual default possibilities of both, how correlated are they, how much excess spread is there in the corporate bonds? Determining the risk-return trade-off between governmental bonds and corporate bonds is a task in a new light. Since governmental bonds actually have a default rate, the game has changed from when we considered them risk-free. It is a trade-off. If the governmental default rates are considerably smaller than corporate bonds there is a trade-off between excess return and security, which must be measured in the light of potentially diversifying away some of the risk. However, perhaps governmental default rates are similar to corporate default rates (which is what I believe is true at least in comparison to investment grade bonds). In this case, governmental bonds are simply low yielding versions of fixed instruments.

This idea that governmental bonds are "simply low yielding versions of their corporate counterparts," is an idea that usually provokes a response. There are generally two classes of reaction. The first says, more or less, "How could you say that! Governmental bonds are special and have great security associated with them." The other reaction says, "Duh, that's why we buy so many corporate bonds."

Which camp are you in?

In the end, a diversified corporate portfolio can have a default rate that for all practical purposes is like that of a (perhaps diversified) governmental portfolio. Let us call the return associated with this level as the "risk-free rate." It is not risk-free as in our naïve view when governments were immune to default. But in a way that accepts the frailties of the phrase "risk-free" to include a default possibility that would be too messy to bring into our practical IRR statements (as discussed earlier). In this sense both the governmental bonds and the diversified corporate portfolio present two different cash flows that have comparable default values. The difference is that corporate bonds have an additional spread that government bonds do not.

What about our diversified corporate bond portfolio making more expected value than government bonds but having the same (or comparable) default risk? Can this make sense in the CAPM methodology? Yes. Perhaps governmental bonds are simply not on the efficient frontier. Maybe corporate bonds are on the efficient frontier, or at least closer.[42] How many times have we seen a bond yield graph like the one below? It is staring us in the face that the corporate bonds are more efficient (in an asset-only way).

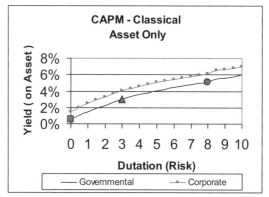

Figure: Typical Governmental and Corporate Yield Curve graph

The idea of two equally risky cash flow streams that have different yields may trouble you. If so, this is due to your studies in modern finance, in which you learned that equally risky streams must have the same return. This is not the case. Economics has a solution to this problem with its supply-demand thinking.

Tip 37: Actuarial science is the middle sibling between the quarrelling brothers: Economics and Modern Finance theory.

There is a fundamental conflict between Economics and Modern Finance. Actuarial science attempts to embrace both sides of the conflict with risk neutral versus real world pricing. I use market consistent pricing as a representative idea from Modern Finance. I use real world projections as a representative idea from Economics.

To illustrate the conflict, I use Black-Scholes pricing formula as an example. Black-Scholes would have us believe that the price of an option arises from the dynamics of the market. The option price is a function of environmental variables (like interest rates), variables of the underlying security (e.g. stock price, dividend yields, volatility) and the structure of the option security (e.g. maturity, strike and option type such as put/call). The conflict with Economics is that the Black-Scholes formula for the option price has no parameter that reflects supply and demand. Economics says that all prices are set by supply and demand. Black-Scholes formula does not even use a parameter for supply or demand. Market Consistent says that markets function as dynamic systems, like those in hard sciences. This is the conflict.

Supporters of the Market Consistent Theory at this point say, "That is not true. Effects of supply and demand are reflected in the implied volatility of the option." However, this view mixes the original meaning of the volatility parameter. The theory's original intent was that this parameter should reflect the underlying volatility of the underlying security.

There is no way to estimate the future volatility (other than to guess). In practice, the volatility has become the "free lever", the open parameter that can be used to calibrate to any option price. Although Market Consistent claimed the price is set by a dynamic market process, like a physical system might be. They even use the same models as relativity. Lacking any other supply-demand variable as required by Economics, the volatility filled this role. Since it was a free parameter anyway with no decisive way of being measured, this had no obvious problem. Finance justifies the arbitrariness of the volatility by vaguely saying supply and demand with the volatility changes in unexplained ways. Do you remember the volatility smile?

This is the conflict. Economics says prices are set by supply-demand considerations. Market Consistent theory uses the arbitrage-free criteria to set prices, and although no one says it directly, the implication is *without any considerations for supply and demand*.

The balance of this argument seems to favour Economics. This is not just because Long Term Capital Management imploded. Black-Scholes' option pricing formula has a free parameter. It is hard to measure. Remember it needs to be future volatility, not recent volatility. In practice, it seems to fill the role of the supply-demand adjustment that Economics requires but finance disavows. One might be tempted to say that Economics is winning this particular skirmish.

However, do not forget that supply-demand is notoriously hard to measure as well. Even though Economics says that it explains all prices, this is only a qualitative model. A conceptual model is near impossible to put into practice.

Market Consistent purports to reproduce prices. Actuarial Science refers to this as risk neutral pricing. (Actuarial Science is not alone in using this name.) In risk neutral pricing, recreation of prices is the ultimate yardstick. A finance model that does not recreate prices has a lot of explaining to do.

Economics attempts to forecast. Its record of achievement may be chequered, but Economics makes no claim that market prices know everything. Economics methods routinely appeal to indicators other than price. Actuarial Science refers to this as "real world" analysis (pricing, projection, etc.).

Actuarial Science sometimes uses the Economics version of things. At other times, it uses the Market Consistent version. For example, in Solvency II there is a requirement that best estimate balance sheet calculations be market consistent (risk neutral). This is a form of Market Consistent theory thinking. Furthermore, we stress the current environment (perhaps rolling forward 1 year) then in the new shocked situation, the balance sheet should be re-estimated in a market consistent (risk neutral) manner. Again, this is Market Consistent thinking.

However, how do we set the stress? What is an appropriate stress to judge a 1-in-200 event, the bread and butter standard for Solvency II capital setting? To judge this, practitioners usually perform historical analysis on how markets have actually moved in

The past. Actuaries call this real world analysis. Others call it Econometric thinking, a branch of Economics. It is a departure from the pricing models of Market Consistent.

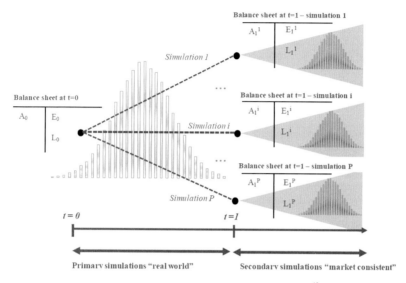

Figure: Market Consistent values versus Real World.[43]

This is a sound treatment. It encompasses the best of Economics and Market Consistent thinking, in the appropriate places.

This is why I say actuaries embrace both arenas, Modern Finance and Economics. Actuaries, and insurers, use both. Horses for courses. Actuaries are the middle sibling between quarrelling brothers. This is not a criticism of these theories intended to throw either of them out. On the contrary, by seeing their differences we can use both. We need to know how and when to use them in order to use them well.

I end this chapter on a further positive note.

Tip 38: Diversification is a true benefit.

We saw earlier that diversification through international markets in equities greatly reduced our capital requirement. (See Tip 12.)

We develop this point further in Appendix 1, Appendix 2 and Appendix **3** with modular models. It is worth mentioning here that this contribution from finance has had great influences on insurance strategy, and rightfully so. Our major tool for reducing capital requirements for insurers is the diversification benefit. As we see later, this benefit comes in many forms, from aggregation all the way down to setting individual stresses.

Chapter 6: Uncertainty is Rife, enough so to justify Simpler Models.

An old adage about Hungarians says that, "A Hungarian can enter the revolving door behind you and come out in front." In my experience, this is true. I have had many fine colleagues in Hungary. In the end, they all seemed smarter than me.

I fell in love with Budapest from the first trip. It was only a matter of time before I moved there. I fell in love with a Hungarian woman and now have four Hungarian children. All of them are smarter than me.

My company had bought the old communist insurance agency, or more accurately half of it. The government divided the old insurance agency into two parts in order to foster competition. The halves were sold off separately. We had inherited all the long fixed pension and annuity obligations. We were literally the only institution in Hungary with long-dated fixed obligations. What to do with them was a challenge for an organization that was just grappling with the issue of being a for-profit business. During the communist era, there were no capital requirements or reserves. It was more of an accounting agency, to see how much money had flowed through the social security system. Asset-liability management was a mere catch phrase when I arrived, an exotic import from the West, like Coke.

The first big problem was the fact that there was no long debt in Hungary. The corporate bond market had not yet developed in Hungary. Foreign big names used their international credit ratings to raise capital much like a vacuum cleaner would suck up cotton candy in a candy store. The local market loved to lend them money. The feeling was that the foreign companies were safer than the local Hungarian government bonds. (See Tip 36.) Still, most of that debt was floating. Investors were afraid of hyperinflation. What were we to do with our long fixed liabilities? How could we match them?

As it turns out, the Hungarian treasury was quite willing to issue "longer paper." We should take this in context. The Hungarian market was issuing 12-month and sometimes 18-month issues. This was not doing much for our liabilities that went out as far as 30 year, albeit on a declining amount. We initially got them to issue us 3-year paper. They loved the 3-year maturity. We loved the returns, with double-digit real yields. Eventually, they got used to the idea of long bonds, and we got even more favourable terms. This is a case like that discussed in the previous chapter: risk is in the eye of the beholder. These were great deals given our situation, but the rest of the market had little need of these long bonds, at least initially. We valued them highly. The rest of the market did not take any notice.

All of this left an asset-liability matching problem. We had the only long paper in our portfolio from Budapest to the border. Still, the structure of the portfolio did not match our declining long-dated liabilities. How should we do an asset-liability match in an environment with no long bonds to use as a benchmark? We discussed and tried out a number of valuation methodologies, using a host of economic scenarios and assumptions. Eventually, the local geeks in my department and the management started getting comfortable with the process. Indeed, they really got the hang of it and started challenging me with what they brought to the table. My Hungarian colleagues were well trained in economics. I was astounded by the innovations that they introduced into what otherwise seems a straightforward annuity matching exercise. I had gone in as an asset-liability management expert, but they were coming out the revolving door ahead of me.

Eventually, these models became more trusted than was warranted. As is typical with these models, it is easy to forget the road you have travelled. It is human nature to lose sight of assumptions made along the way. One day, I arrived back at my office to hear a heated debate between two members of my department. I was not yet fluent in Hungarian at that time, but I got the mood quickly. As it turned out, they were vehemently arguing whether the duration of liabilities was 5.1 or 5.3.[44] Despite myself, I had to laugh.

I sent them to their respective corners, borrowing the boxing imagery, and asked them to review the assumptions of the duration calculation. When you take into account the long-range interest assumptions we made, the mortality variability and other such things, it was easy to see that our liability duration could have been anything from 4.4 to 6.7. A good honest expression of the uncertainty of the estimates we made meant that the argument over 5.1 versus 5.3 was a bit silly. Both estimates were well within the range of feasibility.

It does raise the question of the meaning of the duration match if the confidence interval for duration is so large. In general, we, as an industry, have grown used to point estimates without statements regarding the likely range of that estimate. I discussed this in Tip 34, saying that asset-liability management should use the same model for both assets and liabilities. We were certainly comparing apples to apples. Still there was a wide range of possibilities for the duration match.

Westerners often have an attitude of, "well that's Hungary." In fact, this issue was true in all countries I have worked. Japan is quite an advanced economy. When one correctly accounts for the lapse assumptions of products and the guarantees, along with uncertainty over credited rates, large confidence intervals for duration of liability also appeared, in the range of 4.7 to 5.6.[45] Given the lower interest environment of Japan, this represents the same level of uncertainty. The Hungarian discussion was repeated with Japanese clients when they were having internal squabbles over differences in duration. There again, slight variation in underlying assumptions meant that you could not place an exact figure on duration. I have also witnessed this discussion in Spain, Scotland, England, Belgium, Slovenia, Italy, Australia, The Netherlands and the USA. It is universal.

We routinely ignore uncertainty. We should not. An analysis might say that the fair premium is £100 ±9 with a 95% confidence interval. Most of us stop reading after the "£100." We go on to set the premium at a specific figure. We need one figure after all. All that uncertainty that we mentally scribbled out is still in our capital. Needing to pick a single figure to continue with does not mean there is less uncertainty.

Tip 39: There is a lot of uncertainty in all our capital estimates.

We do not talk about it too much. Few people like uncertainty. Uncertainty is like the family secret we try not to talk about, at least with people outside the family. Nonetheless, professionally we should be honest about what we do not know. The United Kingdom actuarial profession, for one, has included a statement that all estimates must be accompanied by evaluation of their uncertainty.[46] To not do this, is against the professional code. I believe this should be a global ideal for actuaries.

The above example of duration focuses on one of our best estimates: what is the duration now, today, or at least as of the last reporting period end. If that estimate is uncertain, what uncertainty surrounds Solvency II estimates? In particular, how uncertain are

Solvency II capital requirements? This question and its answer will have profound implications for how we make a Solvency II model.

Let us look at a couple of examples.

I use the example of finding the 1-in-200 event equity stress. This is a basic concept of Solvency II. This continues the example used after Tip 12. To simplify it, let us suppose that our portfolio is the FTSE 100. In practice, our portfolio would most likely differ from any particular index. This causes tracking error and basis risk. For this example, I ignore this. Let us assume there is no difference between our portfolio and the index. We can ignore all the other potential risks just to make the discussion workable.

What is the 1-in-200 event for equity prices? It is natural to look at the history of the index prices, to do some analysis, and to come up with an answer. The Extreme Events Working Party[47] group did exactly that. They concluded that the 1-in-200 stress is a percent drop somewhere between 8% and 75%.

"Huh?!" This is a typical reaction when reading this report. If I have a £100 million portfolio, the required 1-in-200 Solvency II capital requirement is £8m, or £75m, or something in between. Perhaps this is not what you were expecting.

The people on this working party are bright. They are not pulling our collective leg. Could we not pin down the number at least a little more than this, please? This seems to take the "Science" out of "Actuarial Science."

The Extreme Events Working Party used a host of models and compared them with a range of assumptions. Part of the range of potential stresses comes from the use of many different models. If we limit ourselves to any one of the models, the range is reduced, but still quite wide.

Actually, any reduction in the range should not be comforting. It required us to choose arbitrarily one of the models used. The original large range encompassed the fact that we do not know the model. Choosing one model, calling it expert judgement, and reporting a smaller range of possible stresses is cheating. Well, it is only cheating if we fail to mention the other methods. If different methods pass statistical muster (as in the case of the distributions used by the Extreme Events Working Party), then we cannot make the uncertainty "disappear" by expert judgement. We must choose a model to use, of course. However, the uncertainty remains. It retains the history of our decision.

"But how can the range be so large?" you might ask. It is important for everyone in Solvency II to have a mental picture of why the uncertainty is so large.

Let us use the FTSE 100 data in a little detail. As mentioned earlier, the worst annual fall[48] was about 50%, actually 49%, in 1974 and the second worst fall was 31% in 2008. The first few results are:

Year	Simple Return
1974	-49%
2008	-31%
1973	-24%
1931	-24%
2002	-22%

The data set I used did not have 200 years of data. However, since Solvency II calculates required capital via a 1-in-200 year event, I will proceed as if my data had 200 years of returns. With this assumption, the worst drop out of our (assumed) 200 years of data is - 49%. The uncertainty that we get in the analysis below is less than one would get in an actual analysis in which we acknowledge the data is not 200 years long. This is a simplifying assumption for this discussion. Still, the uncertainty we see below is enough to demonstrate that uncertainty is high.

Under my assumption, the worst 1-in-200 year event in our history was a fall of 49%. Is this "the" 1-in-200 year event to use in a Solvency II setting? If we use 49% as a 1-in-200 year event, what uncertainty do we have about it? A lot as it turns out.

Suppose this was our 1-in-200 event. What would that mean? If this were the 0.5% quantile in a probability distribution, what could we expect the worst event to be from 200 random years (200 random draws from the distribution)?

I simulated 200 years of returns, based on the lognormal distribution.[49] I found the worst year in this simulation. I repeated this 50 times. I produced 50 different simulated 1-in-200 year events. (I simulated in total 50 x 200 = 10,000 annual returns, taking the worst from each set of 200 points.)

Of these 50 simulated 1-in-200 year events the worst was -56% while the highest worst return -37%. These simulations produce a range of possible 1-in-200 year events, a relatively large range. Of course, in practice, we cannot run the last 200 years over again 50 times to see the result. We only have 1 history of data to look at. This thought experiment is just a way to see how far away a witnessed 1-in-200 year event can be from the actual. The answer is that it can be far away. I simulated using a -49% assumption. But the 50 different histories displayed 1-in-200 year events from -37% to -56%. That is a side range.

Any particular simulation of 200 years can have a worst event that is materially different from the actual 1-in-200 event.

If I chose another distribution, something not Normal, for example a Student-T distribution, I get a similar range of worst returns. The range of 1-in-200 results over 50 simulations is provided below for various assumptions for degrees of freedom (DoF).

DoF	Range of worst in 200 over 50 simulations
3	[-97%, -26%]
5	[-64%, -29%]
10	[-73%, -36%]
20	[-58%, -39%]
50	[-63%, -41%]

The ranges here for the Student-T distributions have wider ranges than the Normal. It should also be emphasized that each of the above ranges represents one result for a sample of 50. Rerunning the samples would produce different ranges.

The Extreme Events Working Party used the lognormal distribution, the Student -T distribution and many more distributions than I have here. The more distributions you try, the wider the range of results you will get. We can see why their conclusions have such a wide confidence interval. Their conclusion was that the 1-in-200 stress for UK equities had the following range:

Extreme Events Working Party: [-75%, -8%]

If you are reading this on the tube or late at night or for whatever reason reading this in a lazy way, you might say something like, "Why doesn't he increase the number of simulations to get a tighter range?" The point here is not to calibrate the 1-in-200 year event from simulations. I do not need to calculate the 1-in-200 event accurately. I know my model uses 49%. What I wish to do with these simulations is to recreate the uncertainty in our history analysis. I am making the point that even if I know the right answer (49%) it is not possible to see it in a simulation. How could I possibly deduce the answer from 200 years of data? Our history of data represents one simulation. The question is how certain is that worst year in that simulation as an estimator of the true 1-in-200 event. How do we know whether its worst event is near the actual 1-in-200 or not? We do not know.[50] The range of possible answers is large.

Let us take this from a different angle. What is the chance that the 1-in-200 year event is better than the worst case we see? The probability of a single year being higher (less onerous) than a 1-in-200 worst event is $\frac{199}{200}$. The probability that each of the 200 years has a return higher than the 1-in-200 year event is $\left(\frac{199}{200}\right)^{200} \approx 36.7\%$. There is a 63.3% chance that the actual 1-in-200 event is not as bad as the worst year we have seen.

This is not decisive either. Although it is more likely that the 1-in-200 is not as bad as we have seen, there is better than a $1/3^{rd}$ chance that it is even worse than we have seen. It is not even perfectly clear (or even slightly clear) if the worst we have seen is better or worse than a 1-in-200 year event.

All of this is uncertain. There is no sound statistical way to reduce this uncertainty objectively.

The above discussion shows that our estimates cannot be exact at all. Suppose our only risk was equity risk and the FTSE 100 represented our risk. If we had £100 million without any liabilities, the capital would be somewhere between £22 and £95 million, assuming a 1-in-200 standard. Even if we accept any particular distribution assumption, like the Normal, the capital range remains wide, from £25 million to £41 million. That is still a lot of uncertainty. The uncertainty gets even more pronounced when we include factors such as reliance on a particular data set, the fact that the data may not represent our risk perfectly, and so forth.

The enormity of the uncertainty is unnerving. It is humbling. We (me too) are naturally open for any solution that would have us avoid facing this uncertainty.

How does this get resolved in practice? Three general activities occur. None of these actually reduce the uncertainty, but it is important to go through them. Even high-level managers need to have a general concept that we cannot do away with this uncertainty.

What are the general methods for reducing uncertainty in practice (staying with the example of choosing an equity stress)?

1. Just pick a stress level.
2. Discredit the most extreme year,
3. Change the statistics to mask the uncertainty.

Taking these in order, we could simply pick a 1-in-200 estimate and call that the figure we need. This is what many people do in practice. Certainly, there is nothing wrong with using a particular estimate. We need a particular estimate to calculate capital requirements, after all. However, often the original uncertainty is simply discarded, forgotten, erased. After selecting one parameter, it is tempting to treat it as "right" and exact.

This view comes in many guises. You can recognize when this method has been employed by paying attention to the words the practitioner uses. A typical expression might be:

> "Selecting the parameters is quite difficult, but then after that the analysis is easy."

This is a typical lead into a Monte Carlo approach. Monte Carlo supporters pick one parameter, like our equity stress above, and then fix it. Equivalently, they might fix a volatility parameter or a distribution. They then go off and do 100,000 scenarios, or 1,000,000, and feel quite satisfied that they have removed (or at least reduced to an acceptable tolerance) any "error" from the analysis. The "error" that they have addressed is sampling error. The uncertainty from the parameter selection remains.

When a rerun with different parameters is suggested, there is usually resistance.

"The model takes too long to run."

"We know it will give a large difference, and only confuse the answer."

There is usually an acknowledgement that the effect would be large. Perversely, this is often used as a reason not to do the test with a different parameter. The Monte Carlo supporters seem to use this argument to "fix" the parameters as soon as possible and for as long as possible. Otherwise, the credibility of the Monte Carlo accuracy might be brought into question. We cannot have that, can we? I revisit this theme in more detail in the next chapter, but just to say it directly, yes we can challenge the result. Without challenging the sampling accuracy, we can say that the uncertainty of the final estimate is large. It is no fault of the Monte Carlo process. It arises from the uncertainty of the parameters. The parameter uncertainty was not removed. The Monte Carlo did not reduce parameter uncertainty. Our focus on Monte Carlo methods only serves to mask the uncertainty around parameters.

Another typical guise is the following:

"Industry surveys indicate that XYZ is an appropriate parameter."

This is the industry-consensus theme. This methodology is relied on more often than makes me comfortable, in all honesty. It is more prevalent in the investment industry where they talk about the "prudent man" rule: a prudent man is a man who acts as other men of prudence do. This is the legitimization of the herd mentality. Do not get me wrong. We do need to make decisions. We do need to choose parameters. Perhaps a consensus methodology is as good as any other (when statistics fail). With agreement in this manner, I do not mind that we select or agree a fixed parameter.

I take exception with the fact that this gives unwarranted comfort. The agreement of the herd causes everyone to forget that there is uncertainty. Agreement can be comforting. However, as Bernard Bosanquet once pointed out, "Extremes of thought may meet in error as well as in truth."[51]

I summarize the above discussion with the following tip:

Tip 40: Fixing a parameter does not reduce its uncertainty.

The next option for reducing uncertainty is to examine the worst year, see what was happening then and ask the question if those types of things could apply today. The conclusion is usually "no," but not convincingly.

For example, in 1974 the circumstances in the UK were unusual, to say the least. As mentioned in
Chapter **4** and Endnote 19, there are reasons to exclude these points as extreme and uncharacteristic of our current situation. Whether or not you accept these, this will actually do little to reduce the uncertainty. If we were to throw out 1974 and redo our analysis, the stress level might be less for our estimate, but the range would still be quite wide. And who is to say that other different conditions might occur with similar effect?

Tip 41: Uncertainty relates to the number of data points, not only the level of the results.

The last plan for reducing uncertainty is to go get more data. This is point 3 above: change the statistics. More data can be good, as long as it really is more data. Unfortunately, there are techniques that superficially look like they reduce uncertainty, but the uncertainty is only masked.

The leading mis-methodology for masking uncertainty is overlapping data, covered in the next tip. The above tip is referring to feeling certain because the answer is comfortable. If we expect a stock stress of 40% and get 39%, we are comforted. It fits in with our intuition. If, however, the 39% arose from only 10 data points, the uncertainty surrounding this estimate should be large. The fact that the estimate happened to be near a comfortable number does not increase the certainty. It does not decrease the size of the confidence interval. The comfortable feeling surrounding the number only serves to mask the true uncertainty.

Tip 42: Do not lust after big N. (Statistics version: Do not use overlapping data.)

This is a particularly technical point and for that reason, I have relegated it to Appendix 1: Overlapping Data. The message here is not to use overlapping data. As I mention in the appendix, I suspect this might be one of the most controversial statements in the geeky word since the use of overlapping data is wide spread.

It is crucially important for executives and managers to be aware that there is large uncertainty in all our estimates, especially the 1-in-200 year estimates. The technical term is "material" uncertainty. This formal term masks the enormity of the issue. From Board member down, everyone must understand the size of this issue and face it directly.

The short version of why overlapping data is bad is given below for those who are interested but not interested enough to read the appendix. There are two points:

1. Consecutive data points from an overlapping data set are not independent. Virtually all statistical tests require independence. It follows that none of our statistical test are valid for overlapping data.

2. To this author's knowledge there is no valid estimate for the error associated with the estimate of a 1-in-200 event. To use an estimate without any indication of its certainty is inappropriate. In the United Kingdom, it is specifically against the Technical Actuarial Standards.[46]

Tip 43: Aggregation carries or amplifies uncertainty.

It is very tempting to hope that this uncertainty issue would just go away. One way is to say, "There are several risk factors, which during aggregation would tend to cancel out the uncertainty." Nothing could be further from the truth.

Uncertainty (wide confidence intervals) relating to specific, standalone risks (equity prices, interest level, etc.) carries over and becomes amplified during the aggregation process.

Let me do a scaled down version to illustrate the point.

Suppose we have two risk exposures, for example interest rates and currency. For simplicity, let us assume our "exposure" to each is 100. Drawing motivation from the equity example above, let us say for illustration that each of our estimated 1-in-200 event has a confidence interval from [-25% to -41%]. I model these as normal variables, with mean -33% and a standard deviation of 8%. This situation so far looks like:

Risk	Exposure	Required Capital – Best Estimate	Range of Required Capital
Interest Rate	100	33	25 – 41
Currency	100	33	25 – 41

The above range represents one standard deviation. If we wanted a 95% confidence interval, the range would be 33±16 rather than 33±8. Using the one-standard deviation range, the width of the confidence intervals is 32 (= 2 x 16), which is the same size as the best estimate itself.

Now, let us aggregate these. I will use a Standard Formula approach with a 50% correlation:

$$\text{Diversified Required Capital} = \sqrt{I^2 + C^2 + 2 \times 50\% \times I \times C}$$

$$\text{Diversified Req. Cap.} = \sqrt{33^2 + 33^2 + 2 \times 50\% \times 33 \times 33} = 57$$

80

If instead of the best-estimate required capital (33), we used 25 or 41, the required estimate varies from 43 to 71. This is a range of 28.

If we used combinations of 16 and 48 (which is 33±16 with rounding), from the 95% confidence interval, the Statutory Capital Requirement (SCR) estimate varies from 28 to 83. This is a range of 55. The range of possible diversified capital requirements in a 95% confidence interval is about equal to the best estimate.

On a percentage basis, diversification has eliminated none of the uncertainty. The range of diversified capital, relative to its size, is just as big as for the individual risk.[52] The conclusion is that aggregation does not reduce uncertainty. This is a simple example, but it is true for more complex ones as well.

We have seen that the uncertainty of individual risks is enormous. We have seen that aggregation (diversification) across risks does not reduce this uncertainty (percentage wise). Can it get worse?

Tip 44: Know that the uncertainty of correlations is enormous. This has large effects on the final required capital.

In the previous capital model with interest rate and currency as the risk, watch what happens if we vary the correlation parameter.

Correlation between r and c	Best Estimate Diversified Capital	95% Confidence Interval of Diversified Required Capital
-25%	40	[21, 60]
0%	47	[24, 69]
25%	52	[27, 77]
50%	57	[29, 85]
75%	62	[32, 92]

This sensitivity of diversified required capital to the correlation assumptions is pronounced.

This would prompt many practitioners to respond, "We simply must be careful when choosing this parameter." We have seen this response before. When faced with uncertainty, just pick one. As said before, this does not reduce uncertainty, only ignores it. We can pick one to develop an answer, but we must not forget the uncertainty of this choice. One manner of denying the uncertainty is just to ignore it and call it expert judgement. A lion can eat an ostrich even if the ostrich sticks its head in the sand.

It is well known that the correlation between two variables (say currency and interest rates, or anything really) varies widely according to the timeframe used to calculate the correlation.[53]

However, this is not the whole story. Even if we knew for certainty the timeframe over which we should calculate correlation, the uncertainty is still enormous. When we calculate "correlation", we are actually calculating an estimate for correlation. However, that estimate also comes with a confidence interval.

There is a rule-of-thumb estimate for the confidence interval of a correlation. It depends on the number of points used. If the number of points in the sample is N, then the standard deviation of for the correlation estimate is roughly $\dfrac{1}{\sqrt{N-3}}$.[54]

For example, if our sample had $N=19$ points, then the standard error would be 25% which is calculated as $\dfrac{1}{\sqrt{19-3}}$. To form a 95% confidence interval, we would double this. Thus, any calculated correlation would have a 95% confidence interval of ±50%. That is a lot of uncertainty in our correlation estimate.

If N were 103 (like a little more than a century of data), then the standard deviation would be about 10% and the 95%-confidence interval for the correlations would be roughly whatever we calculated ±20%. That is still a lot of uncertainty.

This represents another case in which it is tempting to lust after big N. For example, if it were possible to validly switch to monthly data, and N = 103 x 12, then the 95%-confidence interval is our estimate ± 6%. I emphasize that this adjustment is likely invalid. It would be tempting to believe in this tight confidence interval, but it is an illusion. (See Appendix 1: Overlapping Data.)

The wide confidence intervals mean that our required capital estimates are uncertain and in a big way.

Tip 45: Consider Bayesian statistics.

Bayesian statistics focuses on the uncertainty of parameters. Reformulating our models in this light would have two advantages. On the one hand, we would utilize the tools of a main branch of statistics. On the other hand, it would add insight.

I do not want to include a discussion of Bayesian versus classical statistics. That would be a long discussion. It can also be quite lively, as geeky discussions go, since both sides hold strong views. I mention the debate surrounding Bayesian statistics, or if you prefer, surrounding classical statistics, because Bayesian statistics seems underrepresented in the actuarial professional training. A little Bayesian thought may well add a lot of understanding.

My personal view is that actuaries should be able to move back and forth between both types of thinking, Bayesian and classical statistics, using the correct tool for any particular job. This is similar to the situation mentioned earlier in which Modern Finance is at odds with Economics, and actuaries must use both in their work. (See Tip 37.)

As this chapter has shown, our models inherently have large uncertainty. The standard for Solvency II capital setting is the idea of an "accurate estimate of the 1–in-200 event." As we have seen, we cannot make such an accurate assessment. The statistics simply does not support an accurate assessment. In the end, we must contend ourselves with an acceptable 1-in-200 assessment. This is a negotiation. It partly takes place with the regulator and partly amongst ourselves. However, it is important to recognize that we are developing standards of acceptability that we cannot objectively define.

In the next chapter, we embrace this uncertainty in our model strategy. Given that accuracy cannot be an objective goal, we focus on usability. Breaking down the model into bite–sized pieces allows us to manage the model and learn from it. As this chapter has demonstrated, we lose nothing in the process.

Chapter 7: Do Not Use Big Models.

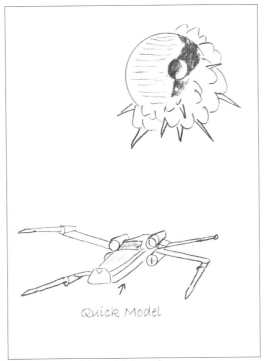

Quick models beat slow ones.

A modern day version of the David and Goliath story is Luke Skywalker defeating the Deathstar in the first-to-come-out Star Wars movie.[55] The nimble fighters slip under the defences of the powerful weaponry to deliver a precisely aimed shot down an exhaust shaft that caused a chain reaction blowing up the Deathstar, the terror weapon of the known universe.

Star Wars and Luke are fantasy (I hope this is not a shock for anyone) but there are points to learn that we can use in real life. Real life fighters on real life carriers work under the same principle. So, the Star Wars analogy works outside of fantasy as well. I could have written my analogy to modern warfare rather than fantasy, but most of us (including me) lack the background to get the analogy. Besides, Star Wars is more fun.

One of the illustrative points is that Luke had colleagues to cover him. Some of those fighters were just a screen (cannon fodder) to buy Luke time to deliver the well-aimed shot. There are no sacrificial lambs in our Solvency II program. At least they have not told me yet, but we can talk about a well-aimed shot. As we discussed in Chapter **4**, you have to have a concept of how to lower capital. Which activities are your well-aimed shot? You must support these activities so that they can have the information and timeliness to effectively lower capital.

On the other hand, a Deathstar is the opposite of a well-aimed shot. Why did the Deathstar fail? The Deathstar was meant to destroy planets. In the end, its flaws and excess power made itself blow up, providing a planet-like explosion not quite intended by the designers.

I draw the analogy to the large systems and processes of Solvency II. I refer to these large Solvency II efforts as Deathstar systems. If an Internal Model system is too cumbersome, it could be a company's death rather than salvation.

It may be well to say again what I mean by a model. "Model" is an all-inclusive term for any system or administration process or decision process necessary to get an answer. "Model" is the sum of all these. The term "Model" does not refer to a particular system or component. Your company may have externally supplied or internally created systems. These form a portion of your model. In addition to specific systems, there may be spread sheets to convert formats from one system to the next, say from an accounting system to a valuation system and back again. These links usually slow the process of running the system. These must be considered an integral part of "the model."

Notice that decision-making processes are included in the model. Even if a system runs quickly but the ensuing committee process is slow, then your overall model is slow. "Model" is not just a systems term. In fact, one externally provided system might work well in one company because the company processes dovetail well with the system. The same computer system in another company could be a disaster because it relates poorly to the surrounding processes.

I use the word "model" in its largest, most holistic meaning.

A model becomes a Deathstar when it cannot aide decision making in a company. When it takes resources all out of proportion to the value it provides, it is a Deathstar. What are the failings of Deathstar models?

Tip 46: Models must be understandable.

Deathstar systems are incomprehensible.

Only after the battle had begun in Star Wars did the Deathstar engineers see the risk, after it was too late. Only after the risk had materialized was it possible to see the flaw in the system. The Deathstar was too complex for their own engineers to see all the risks.

Do you understand the details of your Solvency II model?

That might be a tall order. It might be unreasonable for one person to understand all the details. If you are a manager however, consider the following.

Do you have a map of what all the parts are and who understands each?

This is more to the point. Many of the systems created today give an answer. They may take a quarter of a year to run with no time to do sensitivity checks. It just gives a number, or a bunch of them. As mentioned in the previous chapter, we know that "a number" in Solvency II has a huge uncertainty associated with it.

In fact, it is a requirement of Solvency II that managers (including Board members) understand the model and its limitations.

Does your system do too many things at once?

When I was modelling at EUSI (the insurer that I have not named directly), we were building a new system to meet the then-new regulatory regime for scenario testing. While making sure that we were able to comply with the "New York 7" scenarios required by regulators,[56] we were making a system that could allow any scenario. We limited ourselves to deterministic scenarios, but made sure we could do a lot of them.

What happened? The more we created the system, the more our intuition grew. After time, we were able to estimate surprisingly accurately the answer to a run while the system ran. Of course, our estimates were all back-of-the-envelope. We got so good at it that we had a standing joke, "Why did we build the system if we can estimate this well?" The answer of course was that building the system trained our intuition. By constantly modifying the system and rerunning, our intuition grew naturally. This also occurred in my first job with the annuity writer. Each iteration of our system showed the weaknesses in our thinking and got us closer to understanding. In the end, we were able to continue building the system with features that allowed the most important elements to be tested. We could hand these to the traders to use for transactions. We could develop reports for management that displayed the sensitivities, the limitations.

We could also cut out the unimportant elements. This made the system run faster which meant we could use it more.

We did this by breaking down the system further and further until each piece seemed obvious. My direct colleagues and I were the only ones who saw all the pieces. However, each user could see that his or her piece was complete and doing what it was supposed to do. It was comprehensible in a broad sense: experts could see it worked as a whole, and specialists could see that their particular part was right.[57] We could only achieve this by breaking down the entire system into sub-modules. Each was not too complex for understanding, but sufficiently complex to be accurate enough for everyday use.

Tip 47: Models must run quickly.

Deathstar systems are slow.

When the Deathstar engineers figured out what the rebel fighters were up to in their attack, they saw the danger but it was too late to do anything. They could only offer to the commander the possibility of abandoning ship (which he refused because of pride). By the time a risk had materialized, there was nothing that could be done quickly enough. It does seem that they could have blocked off the exhaust shaft somehow, but big systems are like that: even small changes just seem impossible. Certainly, they cannot be done quickly. It is easier to jump ship.

In EUSI, we made each component easy to change. Traders could change scenarios to test different assumptions relatively easily, for example. These were flexible and easily updated. Automatic market updates further eased our burden. More than just parameters could be changed. When they wanted a new calculation, we had good turnaround time. Quick-running modifications, arising from feedback, kept the sub-modules relevant.

This speed issue was crucial.

The speed of update meant the people could use the system and rely on it. Nowadays, this would go a long way in helping to pass Solvency II's Use Test, even though this was 20 years earlier. By creating a habit of updating readily, the users began to be creative about how they would like to use the system. I do not claim we satisfied every request. Nevertheless, our environment was an open one and the true risks in our transactions and processes were uncovered and addressed over time. None of this would have been possible if the system took 3 months to run, or even a week.

Additionally, bad runs occur. It is a fact of using computers that sometimes a run fails. You must have time to do the eventual reruns to correct errors. You also have to have checks that flag a bad run. This requires intuition about your system and its limitations, what could go wrong. Can you survive a faulty run? If not, then your system is likely a Deathstar.

You should design the sub-modules to be small enough to rerun in the time necessary to use them. For traders this meant a few minutes. For portfolio managers, this could be an overnight run as long as it was possible to update quickly (minutes again, to answer opportunities from the trading desk). Product pricing can take longer, but the quicker the run, the more the pricing expert can test the variability of results and the effects of different features. They can play and learn.

The easiest people to satisfy were the financial reports. They had the longest tolerance for run times. It is interesting to note that in Solvency II, the slowest requirements (reporting) are usually driving the development. This causes them to wonder how they are going to pass the Use Test. If they had started the other way around, providing first to users with the quickest turn around requirements, Solvency II systems might not be running into the speed and process issues that they now are.

Tip 48: Design your models and processes to build intuition.

Deathstar systems give you no intuition.

I have mentioned this above. A typical Solvency II system with large Monte Carlo runs may take 3 months to run, an entire quarter. When it is done, there may or may not have been some sensitivity tests made. Even if there were sensitivity runs, they were all decided at the beginning before any runs, and there is no two-way "what-if…oh, I see, but what if…," type of analysis going on. The answer just comes out at the end, with no ability to modify and see the result.

This slow process means that no intuition develops. Without that, there is no hope of modifying the system to run faster or expose the unforeseen risks. The process simply devolves to a reporting process with little or no risk management. Getting "the numbers out" is already too burdensome.

Tip 49: Models should be inexpensive to run.

Deathstar systems are expensive.

The enormity of these systems cannot be overstated. Some take a computer or array of computers that costs millions of pounds. After these costs come the modifications and the customizations. After all the initial costs, there is need for an army of systems specialists, programmers and some users that you must dedicate to baby-sit the system.

The change process that develops slows down developments further. This leads to a downward spiral of lack of usability leading to more band-aides leading to slower systems leading to less use for anything but the reporting function, leading to less usability, and so forth.

Tip 50: Experts rather than technicians should run systems.

Technicians rather than experts run Deathstar systems.

When looking at nuclear accidents that have occurred in history, it seems that the root cause was ineffective placement of expertise. You cannot hire star physicists to be everywhere. Human resource departments everywhere have a natural pressure to cut corners and use junior staff. This is sound management. Besides, all the great experts would get bored with day-to-day running of a system. However, when a critical incident occurs, this invariably means that the best solution that could have been done, if the experts had been readily available, was not done.

An insurance company is like a nuclear reactor. It can blow up at any time, or melt down, if the right combination of system failures occurs. The nuclear reactor analogy fits in well with the Deathstar analogy.

With a large Deathstar system, there is a business pressure to have more armies of competent people rather than small task forces of experts. The consequences eventually become catastrophic. The Deathstar blew up after all. So did Drexel Burnham Lambert. So did Lehman Brothers, Washington Mutual, CIT Group, Arthur Andersen, Independent National Mortgage, New England Corporation, Conseco Inc., MF Global Holdings, and Enron.[58] I have made no effort to make this list exhaustive, but I think you get the point.

There is nothing wrong with using less trained technicians compared with super-trained experts. I am not saying there is. I am only saying that large cumbersome systems put excessive reliance on technicians figuring out solutions to problems above their pay grade. That is a problem.

If your system were smaller and cheaper, it would be easier to get the experts in the critical places.

Tip 51: Your systems and models must clearly illustrate uncertainty.

Deathstar systems mask uncertainty.

I spent the last chapter emphasizing uncertainty. The bigger the Solvency II system is, the stronger the chance to miss the forest for the trees. The trick is to give every user a garden rather than assign a portion of the forest. As long as people can see their piece clearly, things get noticed that need to be noticed.

At the end of
Chapter **4**, I challenged the idea of "big" as a competitive advantage. If your competitive advantage was being big, then you may not actually have a competitive advantage at all. Large slow systems can lull you into a sense of security. This is especially true for Monte Carlo systems for which proponents constantly emphasize the reduction in sampling error. With the largest military complex in the galaxy, or one of the biggest systems in the insurance industry, a natural complacency develops. I do not mean that people are not busy. Actually, being so busy feeding the requirements of these big systems only serves to distract us from seeing the true level of uncertainty.

For those indoctrinated into the mega-system methodology of Solvency II, it may be difficult to think small. Deathstar designers find fighters too cramped. How does one go about breaking down the huge requirements of Solvency II into bite-sized chunks? How can we avoid the problems given above? How do we make systems that are understandable, that are quick to use and quick to modify, that build intuition with use, that are inexpensive to run and so allow us to have experts manning all the important use points? Furthermore, what do we do about all that uncertainty?

Tip 52: Systems should be easy to adjust to changing requirements.

The Deathstar in Star Wars was defeated because the technicians could not quickly put a lid on an exhaust pipe.

The Matching Adjustment in Solvency II provides a Deathstar analogy. We formerly called this the Illiquidity Premium, but thinking has evolved. Thinking may evolve further. This is a reduction given to some liabilities. Technically, we calculate the liability reduction via a spread over risk-free interest rates when discounting liability cash flows. At the current time, there is not a definitive model. When asked how well their models will be able to handle the eventual Matching Adjustment requirements, most actuaries will get a slightly glazed look in their eyes.

A system must be able to be quickly updated to accommodate changing circumstances. This is true not just for regulatory requirements. Management and decision makers would also like different models to help build their understanding and intuition.

Making such a system would require the right team of experts. This is the topic of the next chapter.

Chapter 8: Team Set-up should be a Pyramid.

Team Work

To set up your model, you need to assemble your team correctly. To set the stage for how to do that, allow me to tell you a tale of two cities. As if I needed to prove that I am not Charles Dickens, my cities will not be Paris and London. Dickens' immortal first line still applies however: "It was the best of times. It was the worst of times."

Melbourne:

One of my early merger & acquisition projects brought me to Australia for the first time. It was exciting. One is naturally pumped up during a potential acquisition. I was young and in the mood to conquer.

I was not alone. While getting off the airplane, I began to meet some of my team members from Northern Europe, the United Kingdom, the USA and other places from far and wide. I had thought it quite a coincidence to be bumping into colleagues at the airport on other arriving flights. It was no coincidence. The "team" assembled was more like a horde. About 80 people converged on Melbourne in the first few days. It would have been almost impossible to not bump into colleagues at the airport. A second wave came a week or so later. We may not have been conquering but at least we were invading.

I was one of three on the investment team. The other teams seemed arrayed in groups of 3 to 5. To this day, I could not tell you what they were all doing. The first day seemed dedicated to settling in and getting over jet lag, with a modicum of introductions. Like most acquisition teams, we stayed up late, told war stories, ate and drank.

On the second day, we did not quite become organized. I do remember the disorder. The football-sized room we were in had a perpetual buzz. "The data room isn't indexed." "Does anyone have a balance sheet?" "How am I supposed to know Australian reserving requirements?" "Have you seen this marketing plan? What a bunch of…." "Who signs-off on consulting hours?" "Where is the org chart for this company?" "We spent over a million euros getting everybody here, you know." "Where's Harry?" "Why don't your trousers match your jacket?" I remember when we found the salary and bonuses paid in the previous year. Some of the most ardent opponents to the deal started warming up to the possibility. "They'll need some help on the accounting. I would be willing to come here."

Every passing day, the pandemonium continued. We outnumbered the local people in the target company, at least in the area we were working. To get time with a manager to ask questions we competed with each other. I saw no progress, no clarity. Days and weeks went by. If someone was getting a clear idea, I must have missed the memo.

Eventually, the Chairman of the Board came to put us out of our misery. The chair typically comes later in the process when the potential deal structure becomes clearer and it might be necessary to start negotiating at the highest level. Since he was coming so early, it seemed clear what he was going to say. "This company is in a big poop." That is not an exact quote. "And if we make a deal, we might be in a big one as well." That pretty much finished the deal. There was some cursory follow up analysis and discussions to be polite. Nonetheless, the decision was made. This acquisition target was a pass.

Looking back on that potential venture, I wonder. Was the target really a big mess? Maybe it was and maybe it was not. Our analysis style was a chaos. We could not have recognized a good deal from a bad. We did not get comfort with the deal. Given the number of cooks, it seems unlikely that that particular broth was ever going to taste good.

Tokyo:

Tokyo was completely different.

More than the mere excitement of a new acquisition, this was Japan. No foreigner had bought an insurance company since the end of World War II. When the war had ended, virtually all insurance companies had been mutualized, no doubt to prevent the occupying forces from taking over share companies. By the time 1990 had arrived, Japan was in the throw of what would later be called the lost decade. The insurance companies needed capital. They looked to the West. We were in the first wave from the West. We could be making history, a point made more than once by our leader. I will call him Lawrence.

Despite the excitement, our response was controlled. Eight of us came the first week, one for each major area: actuarial, marketing, etc. I covered investments. We all reported to the overall head, who was one of the eight. It was certainly easier to book diner reservations than it had been in Melbourne. We were always up-to-date with what happened to each other during the day, or even during the last few hours.

It was easy in that first week to see the issues and develop a broad-based strategy: there was a hole in the investment portfolio; our investment would fill the hole; and we would use the acquisition as a platform for growth that would return our investment and more. All we needed to do was fill in the details.

Being a small group, we had no illusion that we, the initial eight, were going to do this deal on our own. This was by design. Lawrence had a plan. If the project looked like it might work, and it did look that way, we would bring more people in to help. We initial eight were more than scouts. We were the top of the pyramid. As we identified skills that we needed, we brought in the exactly right people. They reported to one of us. Maybe they did not report directly to us, but there was a chain that led to us. It all stayed organized. It grew organically. Even though the team eventually grew to over 150 people on the ground in Tokyo, we always seemed to know what was going on.

After a while, the technical aspect on the investment side did not require me. I was able to go back to my day job in Europe and oversee things from afar. An occasional trip to Tokyo allowed me to keep up-to-date, add strategic guidance, and then get out of the way so the experts who remained could work and feel ownership.

Tip 53: Structure your model-creation team as a fluid pyramid.

Benevolent dictatorship with clear delegation to experts is the preferred method.

A modern aberration of management focuses on consensus. I think consultation is good. Listening is good, too. However, consensus is no way to run a business.

Endless consultation and discussion is not the best way to make a decision. Often it is a cover for not making any decision at all. This effect seems particularly prevalent in Solvency II implementation teams. Since most of the models are new, there is a natural hesitation. We may not know all the ramifications. No, that is not it. We know we definitely do not know all the ramifications. We look around the room. Since everyone else is unsure, the consensus is not to make a decision, "at this meeting." In particular, whoever speaks up and offers a direction will own the decision; when it fails, he knows he will be the sacrificial lamb.

An extreme version of this is most prevalent in Solvency II implementations. More ludicrous than majority rule, some organizations seem to give a veto power to everyone. The slightest misgiving from the least experienced member is sufficient to extend the conversation into another round.

On the other hand, dictators do get things done. Unlike political dictators, business ones can be fired if they get nasty. When given the final decision authority in business, it focuses the mind to make a decision. Since that decision may lead to removal or demotion, there is strong incentive to get it right. However, nobody is expert at everything, nor has anybody time to do everything. Everyone must pass along some decisions, either to SMEs (Subject Matter Experts) or to junior people with the time.

A pyramid is the corporate structure of choice for a reason. Unfortunately, we use a fluid pyramid less often. Companies make an organization chart and stick to it. They assume all decisions fit in that pattern. A fluid pyramid is what I think of for project work, or problem solving. A manager is assigned a problem. Though responsible, the problem is too big or out of his expertise and he cannot do it alone. He delegates sections to people, describing the parameters and goals. In the end, he must approve the final answer, because he knows the context. An initially proposed solution may not work for reasons he nor the junior/expert thought to include in the original formulation. The final decision might take a few iterations.

It is worth emphasizing that when delegating a task, the receiver may not be under the delegator in the company organization chart. The person receiving the task might be higher up. As long as the task has a broad base of support, this should not be a problem. The formal "delegation" may need to go up and down the chain of command to confirm it, but after this step, both can get on with the task at hand.

Tip 53 proposes using a fluid pyramid structure for Solvency II modelling. What does that mean?

Tip 54: Populate the top of the pyramid with the head of the company and at least one expert in aggregate risks.

Aggregation is the greatest benefit to any insurance company. The benefit is so enormous that even companies not particularly interested in generating capital must take this benefit or be insolvent. Aggregation is so important (and so technical) that I have dedicated Appendix 2, Appendix 3 and Appendix 4 to this issue. Since it is the most important capital break an insurance company can get, experts in aggregation must be at the lead of the Solvency II effort. These people must be at the top of the pyramid.

The second layer consists of the individuals identified in Chapter **4**, those people performing the primary tasks that will reduce capital. They must be high enough on the pyramid so that they can voice and address their requirements for using the eventual model.

The third layer consists of all heads of areas relating to risk not covered in the second player. Technically, this third layer need not report to the second layer if there is no logical connection. These players are not strategically crucial (material) for generating capital. They are probably required for the regulatory submission. For this reason, they may have no clear tie in with those on the second layer. These people can report to the aggregators directly. That is okay.

The distinction to make is which elements are necessary simply for Solvency II requirements (3rd level) and which are key areas for potential capital savings (2nd level).

Tip 55: Know the difference between materially large and materially manageable.

Another way to look at it involves materiality. Regulators speak of "material risks." By this, they mean the risk is materially large. However, you can manage some large risks to be lower and some you cannot. I make a distinction between two types or risks. The first type is large but we cannot change them. The second type is large and we can change them. The latter are a different form of materiality: materially manageable. By this, I mean that the effect you could make on the required capital could be large.
Chapter 4 was concerned with identifying which areas of the capital can affect materially manageable risks. We must represent these areas in the second level of the above-mentioned pyramid structure. These are where you can make well-aimed shots to lower capital requirements. In fact, this entire book focuses on materially manageable risks.

For example, longevity may be a materially large risk, but not materially manageable. When you make the longevity model, the required capital may be large but you have no way (no plan) to reduce this. In this case, this would be important to be included in an Internal Model for Solvency II. However, it would not be a driver for generating capital. In this case, this would be a third level risk as mentioned in the pyramid.

However, if your company had a plan to manage longevity that was part of your strategy, longevity could be a materially manageable risk. Your actions impact the size of capital required due to longevity, and this impact may be large. Perhaps you are including postcodes as a differentiating factor, using reinsurance, hedging with longevity swaps or perhaps using Tip 24 from
Chapter 4 for hedging in other ways. In this situation, you should place longevity on the 2nd level, a materially manageable risk.

Risks in the second level, the materially manageable ones, may not correspond directly to risk factors as described in Solvency II literature. For example, hedging longevity risk with pharmaceutical investments would be an activity that does not fit neatly in either the life risk or the investment risk. This is even more reason to identify these risks and to place them in the 2nd level of the pyramid. In that way, we will address them. If the Solvency II risk structure were used, anything not fitting neatly into that structure would get lost.

Tip 56: Make sure any (and all) decision makers necessary for sign-off are in the 2nd layer of the pyramid.

"Will there be places for the current management of my company if we chose your company to work with?" The question hung for a second in the air. It was late at night, after a lot of sake. The question needed to be asked. I was the one who needed to answer it.

On the fourth day of my first visit to Japan, the second-in-command of the target invited me (through various layers of colleagues) to dinner.

Lawrence was mockingly angry. Through grins he said, "I have been coming here for 20 years, sitting in hot tubs and the like, just trying to make contacts, and you get invited to dinner on the fourth day." In good humour, he told me that to be singled out so early in the process was an unusual turn of events, but a good turn.

That night, the four of us, a top man in the target company, a dynamic underling of his (whom I had worked with and come to admire), the translator and myself, had a very pleasant meal. We did not talk about business at all for hours. Then after a pause, the humble question came, "Will there be places for the current management of my company if we chose your company to work with?"

Of course the end of that question was a polite version of "…if your company takes us over?" Apparently, they had been looking for the right person to ask. I was not the lead of the project, and so asking me over drinks was possible. Apparently, my other efforts to respect Japanese business culture were not as clumsy as I had feared. Fortunately, the company I represented was the best in this sense. I could answer, "We would never acquire a company if we did not believe in the management." The conversation quickly reverted to Japanese history, a topic I enjoy.

From that moment on, the acquisition analysis went smoothly. The members of the target company opened up everything to us. We had planted Japanese speakers (Westerners) on our side that pretended they did not speak Japanese while in Japan. These "spies" reported to us that even at awkward moments, underlings would ask how much to tell, and the reply was always, "Tell them everything." Reports and calculations came quickly. We had managed to get the target on our side. They wanted to do business with us.

Notice that the true decision makers were on board early on. In an intangible yet very real sense, the management of the target company was in our decision structure. They wanted to do business with us. We had brought them into the second level of our pyramid, underneath Lawrence. This was not in any formal way. There was no rewritten organization chart. However, they were in a high-level way overseeing events. This is the true fluid pyramid. Without these people, the project would have no chance.

Others on our team were getting other important players on our side. Lawrence had moved mountains to get the Japanese regulator, the Ministry, to accept us as a potential parent. Later when our deal structure had special requirements, the Ministry was agreeable to timely discussions. Our team developed relationships with them early to allow necessary sign-offs to be obtained early. Even if a plan could not get signed-off, then we would know early enough to change our course. We could not put the Ministry on our organization chart either. I am sure they would not have liked that. Conceptually, we must think of them as being there though. They were on the second level of the pyramid with us.

In this sense, the pyramid does not need to be a formal diagram or signed-off document. It may have elements of a checklist of who needs to be contacted and consulted in which instances. It need not formally be constructed, but the leaders in the highest level of the pyramid should be clear about who is in the second level.

In Tokyo in a few short months, we were able to grow the team as necessary, determine what the structure of a new acquisition would be and get everything in Japan set for bringing this company into our group. We figured out who was necessary to buy into working with us and got them on our side.

Well, almost everyone.

In Tip 56, I stressed that all decision makers necessary for sign-off must be brought in the 2nd layer of the pyramid. The final decision of the Japanese project illustrates this, albeit by a negative example.

Despite all the buy-in that we had from players in Japan, our team leader never left his post in Tokyo. Lawrence sent many reports to his home office. However, we were not receiving responses back. "That means they agree," Lawrence would say. After months of reports and documents, and assumption about our strategy, it began to feel strange that nothing was coming back. There was no real engagement.

In the end, Lawrence's Board turned down the proposal. After spending millions on travel expenses and consultants, the answer was "no." A colleague of mine confessed a desire to jump out the window, jokingly of course, though his expression did unnerve me I will admit. After all that time and effort, it did feel like being rejected by your mother. Why did they turn us down?

Tip 57: Strategic support must be positively expressed.

Silence is the easiest way to disagree.

The Board silence in the potential Japanese should have raised warning alarms. It meant that they were not so keen on the way things were going.

Often times in Solvency II projects, as in the rest of business, I read a memo or email that says, "Let me know if you disagree," or words to that effect. In some situations, it is practical not to demand a positive response. In some cases, negative acceptance is fine. This is especially true if the issue is one about which the audience may not really care.

Strategic issues are not like that. Active support is crucial. Without engagement, someone is at best neutral, but more likely dead wood needing to be carried. In the worst situation, the non-engaged party is an opponent waiting for the most opportune moment to object and destroy your plans.

With my tale of two cities, I have illustrated the consequences of not having the proper strategic support positively expressed. Without a positive expression, it might well not be support at all.

I have advocated using a pyramid decision-making structure. The illustration emphasizes that including the right players early on (high in the pyramid) is decisive to the outcome of the project. This underscores the original messages in Chapter 3 (what is your motivation and what is that of the people around you) and
Chapter **4** (before creating the model, determine how it will be used to generate capital). If you have done these initial preparations correctly, it should be direct to continue on to the creation of the model.

Chapter 9: Typical Concerns Anticipated

"Did we miss anything?"

"Our job is not to find a thousand reasons not to do this deal. Our job is to see if there is any way to do this deal that makes sense."
-"Lawrence" leading our Acquisition Analysis

There are two types of objections: those that are said and those that are not.

"The elephant in the room," is a phrase referring to the unspoken thought on everyone's mind. These must be addressed as directly as any spoken concern.

On the other hand, there are concerns that are quite verbalized. Many people find it is easy (and fun) to throw up objections and obstacles. However, I found that the best players see problems much as everyone else does. The difference is they see ways around them.

In either case, you must identify objections and address them. This chapter lists a few typical concerns and addresses them.

Tip 58: (Objection) Cost: Remember the spiral of capital savings.

How many times in my career have I heard cost as the main objection to a new system? All businesses need to reduce expenses and insurers are no exception. Budget controls are by necessity tight. Whenever a major new project comes up, it feels like an assault on budget discipline. Partly this is because the numbers are unfamiliar. Partly it can be because after scrimping pennies, the big expenditure seems to be "throwing away" the savings. That past budgetary discipline may have been painful. Some might view the situation as "throwing away" all the hard work of the past. Nothing could be farther from the truth.

Through all of this, remember the goal.

Remember the possible capital savings. (
Chapter **4**)

Remember the spiral of capital savings. (Tip 1)

Our prospects for generating insurance capital are brightest when we compare any systems outlay, training, hiring to the capital savings. If the case is not compelling, then perhaps you should review your reasons for wanting to generate capital. (See Chapter 3.)

Look at how business-as-usual processes may benefit. There is likely a reduction in on-going valuation expense and other process expense because of the savings incurred by faster systems. The costs are not lost costs. They are investments with high returns.

Tip 59: (Objection) Cost: Consider people who will work for "free" or at least for results-based compensation.

If the potential costs still seem daunting, consider employing people or vendors willing to work at a reduced (or no) fixed fee but get a proportion of the capital savings. This may ease the budgetary squeeze while still allowing you to retain the best talent. Some of the gains are given up, but the initial outlay is mitigated. This seems a good trade, having your cake and eating it too.

If generating capital is not exactly your goal, rather only a tool towards your goal, then adjust the incentive to be in line with your goals. For example, suppose your goal is increasing assets under management. Then make an incentive related to that. If your goal is growth of assets over your current target, then make the incentive kick-in only when assets get and stay over a target formula.

Whatever your goal, remember that there is a tremendous synergy when everyone has the same goal. If we all are paid when capital is reduced, then capital will be reduced. Sharing the reward later may help pay for it now.

Tip 60: (Objection) "It will never work."

There are two flavours to this objection:
1. We can never get the capital savings we envision.
2. It simply will never work.

The first is a natural doubt that may crop up. The solution is to review Chapter **4**, the ways in which you plan to generate capital. These should be independent of any system. If you have a strong understanding of how your business does or can manage capital, you should be able to see that the capital savings will materialize.

The second objection comes up some times. Remember Tip 31: Risk $\neq$ Return. The Board said no simply because the analysis showed too much profit. "It can't be right," is a typical expression of this view. These reactions are not looking at the information. These are prejudicial comments, that "nothing" will work better than what we have already. These comments assume we are on the efficient frontier, which we have seen may not be true. It is most likely not true when people rely on the above assumptions. By assuming there are no chances to improve profits, they stop looking for improvements. By not looking, they practically assure that your portfolio is not the best it could be. The paradigm that Risk = Return is self-defeating. When there are no improvement possibilities by saying, "It can't be true," they are guaranteeing improvement possibilities are there.

I am one for listening to my instincts. I let any nagging doubt encourage me to do more analysis. However, there comes a time when we have analysed it "7 ways to Sunday" as an old boss used to say. If all your analysis, which employs knowledgeable people with adequate time to prepare and consider, says, "Yes," and someone is still saying, "No," then perhaps that person just loves the word "No." When they have no concrete reason to disagree, perhaps they should not.

Perhaps the people saying "No" have no reasons to generate capital. You should review the sections on knowing your allies and colleagues in Chapter 3.

Tip 61: (Objection) We are too late for IMAP (regulatory application for an Internal Model).

The Internal Model Application Process (IMAP) is the procedure that an insurer takes with the regulator in order to get an Internal Model approved. As of this writing, many insurers have already entered the IMAP process with their primary regulator. If you are worried that you have missed the deadline, fear not.

On the one hand, even if a company installs an Internal Model after the first wave of Internal Model applicants, the later comers will probably get the benefits at the same time. You see, for the first few years, all companies must run the Standard Formula. This is a regulatory requirement. Even if you have an Internal Model, you are still required to run the Standard Formula in parallel. It seems unlikely that significant capital savings are allowed if the Standard Formula gives a higher Capital Requirement than an Internal Model. The regulators will simply go for the higher requirement, at least initially while still getting used to the new regulation themselves.

Companies that implement an Internal Model later will have an advantage. A few years hence, we will all have more familiarity with these models. This is particularly true for the regulators. They must get used to the new paradigms, and they will naturally be conservative initially. However, after they have experience, the model made by later entrants will benefit.

On the other hand, many capital savings take place in the Standard Formula aggregation. Many of the methods in
Chapter 4 only require asset changes and would have lower capital requirements even in a Standard Formula setting. In this case, you are not late at all.

Tip 62: (Objection) "But we already have systems in place."

Perhaps the current systems work perfectly well. The methods presented in this book are not entirely different from those currently in the industry.

Perhaps small adaptations are necessary. Perhaps all of those scattered spread sheets are in fact portion of a modular model. You might simply have to bring it all under control to reap the benefits.

Alternatively, a portion of this argument could be a cost issue. It could be a management issue. It could also be that, unlike Tip 61, you already have an IMAP system or at least a portion of one.

There is a subtle cost notion, the idea of sunk costs. A typical phrase regarding sunk costs goes like this, "But we have already spent so much on system/method X. How could we switch to Y?" This is a reputation issue disguised as a cost issue. All decisions should be forward looking. We cannot unspend already spent money. If a change makes sense in a prospective manner, then we should do it, even if it means reversing a past decision. Unfortunately, large organizations, or even medium ones, do not "reverse" very well.

Think hard about a cost argument. Is it prospective or retrospective? If it is about already spent costs, the issue may really be a reputation problem. They do not want to change a decision. If you find your colleagues doing this, or you find yourself doing this, you must address the change in a positive, blame-free manner. "New evidence leads us to…" "Our expectations concerning the vendor have not been borne out." "New technology…" "New industry thinking suggests…." Spin it not to be a reputation issue. It should not be. If pride or fear of blame is causing resistance to change, then the issue should be dealt with specifically.

I repeat the advice from Tip 58 concerning costs. Even if cost is not the exact issue (perhaps management time instead) the lesson is to keep your eye on the ball. Remember, why you wish to generate capital. (See Chapter 3.) As long as any change makes sense prospectively, and it supports yours and the company's strategy, it should work.

Another subtle version of this objection surrounds discussion concerning Business-As-Usual (BAU). Many Solvency II implementations are done separately from the "normal" operations of the company. Companies bring in outside advisors for development. This is fine. The difficulty is the transition to take new methods into BAU processes.

Insurers historically have never made huge changes in their structures. Stable systems and processes have treated insurers well. This may be a defining characteristic of insurers, particularly so for large ones.

Solvency II requires radical changes. Insurance managers must employ skills for rapid change. They may never have done that before. Most were never trained that way. Decisive overhauls of companies are not the main stay of executive skill sets in insurance. Advisors can take some of the workload off BAU for design. However, BAU must be involved, the earlier, the better. Otherwise, the designed solution may be unnecessarily different from the current processes.

Recall Chapter 8: Team Set-up should be a Pyramid. You must bring in all people who are important to managing capital and freeing it up. Bring them in at the second level of the pyramid. Bring in other players for different parts of the model in at the third level. BAU should be represented in the first three levels of the pyramid. There may be need for advisors at the top of the pyramid. However, lower down they may only come in at the fourth level.

Furthermore, with the staged methodology, Appendix 3, there is no need for one big system. We have divided the whole problem. We divide and conquer the problem. Some modules might have new systems. Others might not. Since the BAU managers that will eventually use the systems are part of the process, the question of new systems is local to their own workflow. They likely will be interested in what is the easiest way for them to do their own part.

If you find people clinging to the current systems, you may wish to review their buy in. See Tip 8, Tip 9, Tip 56 and Tip 57.

Tip 63: (Objection) The transition would be difficult.

Typical questions here might be, "Who could we get?" "What new training would be involved?" There are cost questions too which we addressed above.

At least this objection is not negative. Difficult is not impossible. By saying that a transition would be difficult, we have already gotten to the question of how to do it.

If the right decision makers are in place, Tip 8, Tip 9 and Tip 56, and they have indicated their support proactively, Tip 57, then this argument about transition should not really come up. All the above comments about BAU apply. If it is coming up, you might try to place that person conceptually into one of the above tips. This will indicate how to interact with this person. Perhaps that area is not as crucial or committed to capital reduction as you had originally thought. Perhaps they originally thought their commitment was greater. Perhaps they are still committed.

Maybe, this person's commitment is not a problem at all. These statements about difficulty are most likely sincere engagement in the process of change. A problem that is recognized is a problem that is 90% solved. If you see people finding issues in implementation, perhaps that is good and perhaps it is your attitude towards the feedback that needs to be improved.

Tip 64: (Objection) "These methods are untried."

One argument against implementation is that the methods are untried.

In this aspect, modular systems are crucial. By breaking the overall model into bite-sized chunks, we can test each piece separately. They can be tried out and in so doing become "tried" methods. Remember
Chapter **4**. The methods for generating capital should be clear before making the models. In this manner, a blast of "untried" accusations has less wind in its sails.

In contrast, large Deathstar type systems, by their nature, can only be tried in combat. To use them requires a leap of faith. If you have avoided the Deathstar mentality, your methods should already be tried or easily tested. The homework in Chapter 3 and Chapter **4** have anticipated these concerns.

Chapter 10: Systemic and Miscellaneous Tips

Think outside the box for better solutions.

Some of the solutions to capital management lie outside of your own company. For that reason, this is a bonus chapter is included with some systemic and miscellaneous tips.

Systemic tips are ones too big for a single company to handle. One such tip comes up as an entire appendix, **Appendix 4**. It is worth repeating here.

Tip 65: (Systemic) Develop stronger methods for formula fitting losses.

I have mentioned in Endnote 109 and the discussion after Tip 94, the UK Institute and Faculty of Actuaries has set up a working party to study the general loss function. This is an example of an issue that has proved larger than any single company. Despite the number of companies using formula-fitted loss functions for their Monte Carlo implementation, the best approach appears illusive. Indeed, the loss function appears to be the weak link in the Monte Carlo chain. The industry is recognizing this.

My personal view, without having a solution, is that a good method would consider commutation functions for the different risk factors.[59]

Tip 66: (Systemic) Rethink the implementation of the 1-in-200 paradigm.

I like the 1-in-200 paradigm as an ideal. It focuses us to think about the risk we have taken and to consider how they interact. We should avoid the idea of a 1-in-200 <u>year</u> event, and rather focus on the idea of a 0.5% probability event. This side steps the issues of whether we have 200 years of data and if that data is applicable to today's world. This distinction is rather widely understood. So, with this caveat, the 1-in-200 paradigm is sensible.

The part to rethink is our attitudes towards the uncertainty surrounding an estimate. Chapter 6 has illustrated that the level of uncertainty in models is quite large.

The modification that I would like to see in our thinking surrounds the accuracy we subscribe to our estimates. Given that the actuarial profession prides itself on the use of numbers, perhaps it is a natural tendency to overstate the certainty of our conclusions. As seen in the estimates in Chapter 6, the uncertainty surrounding an estimate in a 1-in-200 event is considerable. Our base estimate of 299 for the stock portfolio compares with a range of 105 to 533. This represented parameter uncertainty only. Simply to say the 1-in-200 loss "is" 299 clearly misrepresents the situation. Perhaps we should include "hubris" as an operational risk factor.

I word the rethink in the following way: "Since our estimates have large uncertainty around them, how do we choose a final figure?" We cannot have a capital requirement "between 105 and 533."

This is an area of expert judgement, of course. "Aha," you might say. "Now we have a name for the issue." However, the regulations speak of a "falsifiable test," that could be applied to substantiate the reasoning in an expert judgement. This falsifiable test appears as a defining characteristic of any expert judgement. This does not sound like it covers the uncertainty issue. Decision making in the face of uncertainty is by its very nature uncertain and not falsifiable by known methods.

Uncertainty does not lend itself to a falsifiable test.

This is a loosely understood area. Until we clarify how to make decision in uncertainty, we will all have a tendency to try to prove our numbers are "right" rather than having a serious discussion of a figure's uncertainty and the management implications. First, we have to confess to the uncertainty. Then we can address it.

Tip 67: (Misc.) Change Solvency II regulation not to penalize holding extra assets.

This tip for regulators follows from Tip 11: Pay out in dividends any Own Funds. In Tip 11, we saw that having capital in excess of required capital actually increase the required capital. This is a conceptual error in the regulations. Given that it arises from a technical point, the Delta-NAV calculation in combination with the "whole balance sheet" approach, I feel this was an unintended effect. If a company holds excess assets, who would want to penalize them?

The solutions to this could be easy. Excluding Own Funds when performing the stress is one way. Then any Own Funds would not contribute to the Delta-NAV. Another way might be to move to a calculation that focuses on shortfall of assets versus liabilities. This might be more of a paradigm shift, but it would be a conceptual improvement.

There are no doubt other solutions. My point here is not to solve the issue, but to raise awareness that it should be addressed.

With the next tip, we focus on what a company could do by itself for a specific issue regarding the modelling of joint distributions (copulas).

Tip 68: (Misc.) Consider using an empirical joint distribution.

Consider a situation with two risk factors. One way to model their joint distribution is with an empirical distribution.[60] These are not as fancy as the more famous analytic copulas (e.g. t-copula) but given the low amount of data available to calibrate a joint distribution, empirical copulas do not appear to have any less certainty. This is particularly true for market data. (See Tip 42.) Furthermore, with a tangible joint distribution in hand, questions about tail dependence are easier to formulate and answer.

If used for two risk factors, an empirical distribution can be calibrated. As the number of risk factors increases, the data becomes proportionally more sparse. The empirical fit suffers. With a staged aggregation, this sparseness can be limited by reducing the number of risk factors in each component.

When used in conjunction with a staged aggregation methodology, the empirical joint distribution can be quite powerful. In an extreme case, we can stage the model so that only pairs of risk factors are considered together. Then the empirical joint distribution has its best fit. We maintain all the benefits of staging. Fitting the distribution becomes more automatic. Furthermore, the piecewise linear nature of the empirical distribution lends itself to very quick runs. (The downside is that you may not always be able to arrange your risk factors so that each stage has only two risk factors.)

Tip 69: (Systemic) Develop aggregate asset projections for the industry.

All the insurers are developing independent asset models. If ever there were a project in which shared resources would be beneficial, this is it. Developing large databases individually for each different insurer cannot be efficient. Perhaps a "cloud" computing application could be developed for partner insurance companies that agree to cooperate.

Even if a full-blown joint asset model proves infeasible, there would be benefits for agreement on basic things such as developing a universal protocol for CIC codes that identify assets. You see, there is not even, as yet, a standardized code for referencing assets.

Tip 70: (Systemic) Develop more vanilla derivatives through the exchange to lower counterparty risk.

Counterparty risk can be a large capital requirement. In Solvency II, this has two flavours: Reinsurance counterparties and derivative counterparties. This tip focuses on the derivative counterparty risk.

Insurers use derivatives to manage risk and generate a lot of capital in so doing. Giving up these asset-liability management strategies would be a step backward, causing increased capital. It would be desirable to find ways of doing these derivative transactions without the counterparty risk.

Derivatives in which the counterparty is another company, typically and investment bank, incur a capital charge. Derivatives through the exchange do not.[61] The plan is easy in concept. Put more through the exchange.

However, the exchange does not always have the desired structure. Even non-standard contracts can be placed through the exchange, though it causes more work. My point here is that the paperwork involved is easily justified by the capital savings. Developing the increased offerings requires some industry-wide coordination. This would need to be done with the investment banks and the insurers together.[62]

This is of course, a long-range goal. It would take effort to have the infrastructure to allow more derivatives through the exchange. The rewards would be great. The Spiral of Capital Generation applies here. If we have saved capital with other methods in this book, then we would have the resources to dedicate to longer-term, high-payoff projects like Tip 70.

Tip 71: (Misc.) Use Negative Capital Attribution.

I have not talked much about attribution. I included it as Step 8 of the aggregation process in Appendix 2. It is not crucial for determining the aggregated (diversified) capital estimate.

The attribution methodology is important, however, for the acceptance of the capital model within and organization. Let me explain.

Aggregate capital (loss) must be attributed down to business unit and to risk factors. This is regulatory requirement. The difficulty is that, although done for regulations, companies try to use the attributed capital for management purposes.

Several attribution methodologies have been recommended. I go into none of these here. Most of them are proportional attribution in some manner. Euler is proportional to the marginal standalone capital. Another method is proportional to the actual standalone capital. I am sure there are others.

The difficulty with the attribution methodologies that I have seen is this:

Tip 72: Realise that the attribution of diversification benefits produces capital figures that must be ignored.

By its very nature, the idea of attributing diversification benefits down to business units produces capital figures that inherently must be ignored by managers.

Allow me to illustrate the reason for this via an example. Consider two managers of two business units, A and B that are aggregated up to C.

Given that there is some diversification benefit, the capital for aggregating A and B, is less than the sum of the individual capitals for A and for B. There is a diversification benefit. This is different than the aggregation that A and B may have by themselves. The aggregation at C is over any above any aggregation that may have arisen from A and B alone.

In a typical set-up, the capital savings is attributed back to business units A and B.

To illustrate why the attributed capital must be ignored, consider the following. Suppose from one period to the next, business unit A does not change at all, but that B changes considerably. The change in B is sufficient to change the aggregate capital. In so doing, this changes the net attributed capital back to both A and B. A's attributed capital has changed through no action of its own. The attributed capital at A cannot be indicative of that manager's performance. It moves independently of A's actions or situation.

Managers know this. Everyone knows this. Even people who developed the attribution model know this. Because of this, everyone will stop paying attention to the attributed capital to A and B. It is not indicative of what the managers are doing. Since it does not reflect the situation of the business units, it will be ignored at best. The management noise caused by the fluctuations in the attributed capital will be a distraction. Perhaps it will be used in a perverse way. It could be used politically by less scrupulous managers with a particular angle. The attributed capital will not add management information in any way, and may well distract from important things.

The solution is this: do not attribute any capital reduction to A or B. None. Leave the reduction in capital at the aggregate point, at C. This means that C has a negative attributed capital.

This treatment is not yet standard. In fact, I do not know of any place that does this. Nonetheless, it makes perfect sense. The manager at C is the one making the allocation decisions for capital to business units A and B. By attributing the savings to C, the capital effect is attributed to the manager making the decision. That is proper.

111

The calculations take a little getting used to. Since C has a negative capital allocation, her return requirement is negative. Effectively she is allowed losses. These "losses" are the return on the sum of the standalone capitals for A and B less the diversified capital. These "losses" are the foregone return on the diversification benefit, the capital that we did not use. A is judged by her standalone capital requirement. B is judged by hers. C is judged on the diversification benefit in action. These losses at C "support" the negative capital represented by the diversification benefit. The allowed losses are the reduction in return requirement given to A and B. C is the one deciding the return required from A and B. C is in charge of the reduction required for A and B together. She should manage the reduction in return due to having less capital required.

It all works out. As I said, though, it takes a little getting used to.

Tip 73: (Misc.) Do not calibrate standalone risk to the 99.5% loss level.

All aggregations essentially have each risk driver at a loss level that in a standalone basis is less that 99.5%. If you have ever seen a killer scenario, you will know that each risk factor is at a more mild level than its standalone 99.5th quantile level. One might be at the 80% level, another at the 95% level and another at the 52% level.

It would be better if these levels were the most accurate. Focusing on the levels actually used in the killer scenario makes sense. Of course, rather than for a killer scenario, we should do this for the Curve of Constant Loss. This means that we do not pick a particular quantile for each risk factor for calibration. It does mean that we need to focus on more than just the 99.5th quantile.

Tip 74: (Misc.) Map out "Decision Flow" in your company like computer scientists map out data flow.

It is one thing to map the flow in your organization of data and the processes data goes through. Computer programmers are particularly good at this. This methodology works well when the processes are set and repeated on a regular basis.

We can perform a similar exercise with decisions throughout an organization, even non-periodic ones. All too often, not enough time is given for decisions and thinking. The assumption seems to be that when a report is finished, so is the accompanying decision. This is rarely true.

When one truly accounts for the way we make decisions in practice, the world looks quite different. Reports are sent back for revision or a change of assumptions. Further data needs to be collected (e.g. news or external reports). If your strategy involves finding new markets (like a mergers project) or new investments (like the alternative investments mentioned in this book) then the decision process needs to be fluid. This provides even more reason to determine who the decision makers are and the process by which a decision may be made. No doubt, this process may change over time. Nevertheless, it is easier to see if a developed process needs modification than it is to rediscover or reinvent a process with every decision.

Understanding decision flows is different from understanding data flows. Focus on the true decision making process. Who are the real decision makers? How do they make decisions? Get to know it well.

Tip 75: (Misc.) Develop new products that diversify into new risk factors.

Diversification remains one of the best tools for generating capital. See Tip 38. Branching out into new areas pays off with capital savings. Here is one idea:

Commodity-based pensions:

A defined benefit pension that does not have a fixed cash amount or one linked to an inflation index. Instead, fix it to an energy price, like a gas price. A person, couple or family, would buy so many litres of gas. The insurer would not deliver the gas, but rather would pay the then current price of those units of gas. The policyholder still buys the gas from a provider. A family can well estimate how much gas they would need in a month or year. They can then buy how much they need, perhaps with a little extra just in case. This is a true pension benefit. The policyholder can rest assured that his or her gas bill will be paid.

For the company, after hedging the gas price, this looks like another annuity product. For sure, the hedge would be rather technical since there are no long dated hedges for gas prices. The company would have to hedge through the short market for the gas risk and the long swap interest market for the annuity-pricing piece. Further technical issues arise but we can address each in turn.[63]

Perhaps what works for gas can work for electricity. Perhaps it can work for food as well. (There are plenty of hedge instruments for staple food prices.) A specific policyholder could buy so many unit of gas, so many of electricity and so many of food. The right combination of these could insurer that the policyholder will always have the amount needed for necessities. It there are remaining funds after the necessities are covered, the remainder could be a standard fixed or inflation-linked pension.[64]

This would be a truly comforting product for pensioners. Their true living costs would be protected. They could rest assured.

The insurer would benefit as well. The entry into new risk factors would automatically reduce overall aggregate capital.

Tip 76: Develop multi-company solvency requirements.

With quick models that are accurate within the tolerance set by our uncertainty, we may consider solvency requirements for groups of companies. Reasons for doing this are:

1. Groups of companies could pool overall risk (via some form of agreement) in order to:
   a. Lower overall capital requirements,
   b. Offer a "super-guaranteed" product guaranteed by more than one entity.

2. Pension funds could band together.
   a. If we apply Solvency II standards to pension funds, it is generally accepted that defined-benefit funds would have capital strain. A pooling of risk and capital requirements (as in 1, above) would reduce the relative capital requirement associated with the killer scenario of a single sponsor or groups of sponsors becoming insolvent.

3. A regulator could model an entire insurance industry in its jurisdiction.
   a. This could ascertain where many (all) insurers are "leaning in the same direction" with regard to risks.
   b. Industry-wide requirements could be adjusted according to the risk of industry-wide (systemic) risk rather than formulated on a company-by-company basis.

4. Industry issues could be cast in a wider economic light.
   a. For example, to what extent do insurance credit risk requirements cause a flight of investment capital away from the credit markets? This would cause larger economy-wide ramifications.

Of course, there are problems to cooperating among competitors. How do you maintain competitive "distance" while gaining on areas of mutual benefit? This is a hard question to answer. The rewards could be great, however.

Tip 77: (Systemic) Solvency for individuals: systemic risk associated with the common person.

We should analyse the general population in a Solvency II paradigm. I have left this issue to the end, since it represents an expansion of the Solvency II methods to new areas. Actuaries can play crucial roles on wider social-political scene.

Most individuals would not survive a Solvency II capital assessment. Perhaps they should be able to, at least on average. The lack of survivability of individuals ranks as a systemic issue, bigger than most companies, and even bigger than most governments.

An argument might be that a single individual going insolvent does not represent a risk to the overall system. I submit that the issue is not the potential insolvency of an individual, rather the population in general. The events that make one individual insolvent often are highly correlated with other individuals. While one individual's solvency may not be a systemic problem, the potential for larger portions of the population to go insolvent at the same time does represent a systemic risk. It is a big systemic risk.

For example, in the UK, residential mortgages are usually fixed for only 5 years at most, often only 2 years. If there is a period of high inflation (say 20%), for a couple of years, this would no doubt bleed in to interest rates and raise the mortgage payments on large portions of the population. That is a problem. It would also occur at a time when the typical person was having other problems, such as other prices rising. That is a problem raised to the second power.

I am not saying that inflation will definitely hit in the UK. I am saying that it is a reasonably likely event, probably more likely than 1-in-200. Managing the risk of this event is a systemic issue. Solvency II methodologies may help.

We could perform a balance sheet and risk assessment for sample families or other entities (such as small businesses). We could analyse these via all the tools of Solvency II and those presented in this book. By analysing the "killer scenarios" for the general populace, its Curve of Constant Loss could point to potential systemic solutions.

Of course, simply requiring more capital from the populace does not represent a viable solution. The overall goal of such analysis differs from Solvency II's capital requirement focus. Nonetheless, the identification of risks and quantifying and reducing the conceptual costs of managing those risks may prove useful. Maybe it leads to policy recommendations. Maybe it leads to new products. Maybe the populace has a risk that offsets ones that insurers, pension funds or other industries have. They could hedge each other.

Wouldn't that be fun?

Last Chapter Wrap Up

If you have been paying attention, you will have noticed that this is the end of the last chapter and the number of tips so far is not what was promised on the cover. Don't fear. The remaining tips are contained in the appendices.

The last,

Appendix 5: **Tips by Category**, orders the tips by general topic as a reference to readers.

The first four appendices contain tips that are technical in nature involving how to build a capital model. These are aimed at the more technical audience. The focus is on making models more believable and credible, while also making them quicker and more efficient to use.
However, even without the appendices, you no doubt have some ideas that may work in your organization, and have a concept of how to put them in place. I hope you find these ideas as inspiring as I do.

So, get out there and start your own Spiral of Capital Generation.

Appendix 1: Overlapping Data

The text mentions that your analysis should not use overlapping data:

Tip 42: Do not lust after big N. (Statistics version: Do not use overlapping data.

This is a point where I will likely receive opposition from the industry. Many people in Actuarial Science use overlapping data analysis. This is also true for other industries as well, most notably investment and finance. The widespread reliance on overlapping data analysis may make practitioners comfortable, but that alone does not prove it is valid.

I will get to the specifics of overlapping in a minute, but first let me talk about our love affair with "Big N".

When faced with big numbers, there is a natural awe. "Billions and billions of stars," was an expression that Carl Sagan was famous for saying, and it illustrates the wonder of things.

In scenario testing of financial simulations, we can get carried away with Big N Fever. To test more and more scenarios to eliminate simulation error without acknowledging the uncertainty of the scenario set-up (the parameters) can lead to spurious accuracy and over reliance on the output of the model. A million scenarios, as mentioned above can sound bold, audacious, conquering, so much so that it may blind us to the fact that while the Big N dexterously handles one problem (simulation error), it does not even address others. Parameter uncertainty is one such problem that is left unaddressed with simulations with high numbers of scenarios.

Before any model is run, when trying to address parameter uncertainty, it is natural to gather data, and as much of it as you can. Returning to the example in the text, in an effort to have more N in our historical data set that has only 200 years, we could move to higher frequency data. If we used monthly data, we would have 12 times as many points. If we use daily data, we would have more than 250 times as much data! (Notice how the exclamation point just creeps into the sentence when we get more data.)

The thinking is that with more data points, there is less uncertainty. In statistics, more data leads to a lower statistical error, tighter confidence intervals and less uncertainty. Surely, that applies here. Right?

Not really.

It turns out that using higher frequency data has a marginal advantage, for technical reasons. As a rule, however, we can say that higher frequency estimates lead to no reduction in uncertainty. That is right. I said, "No reduction in uncertainty."

Supporters of overlapping analysis have told me, "It helps with the point estimate. But we don't know how to estimate the error to this estimate." My view is that a point estimate that has no estimate of its accuracy (its potential error) is unusable. The UK actuarial profession also indicates that all estimates must be accompanied by an estimate of their reliability. (Endnote 46.) I take this as support of my position.

Let us consider doing monthly analysis to illustrate the issues. The following table shows how we could convert monthly price data into annual return data using monthly data. Since the first month price is end of January 1900, the first annual return we can calculate is at end of January 1901. We refer to this as a January-to-January return. Then next is a February-to-February return, and then a March-to-March return and so on. In the table, this leads to a new annual return for each month end. We sometimes refer to this as the "rolling annual return."

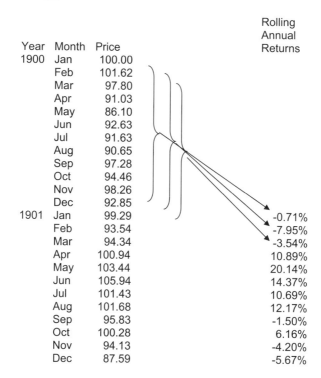

Year	Month	Price	Rolling Annual Returns
1900	Jan	100.00	
	Feb	101.62	
	Mar	97.80	
	Apr	91.03	
	May	86.10	
	Jun	92.63	
	Jul	91.63	
	Aug	90.65	
	Sep	97.28	
	Oct	94.46	
	Nov	98.26	
	Dec	92.85	
1901	Jan	99.29	-0.71%
	Feb	93.54	-7.95%
	Mar	94.34	-3.54%
	Apr	100.94	10.89%
	May	103.44	20.14%
	Jun	105.94	14.37%
	Jul	101.43	10.69%
	Aug	101.68	12.17%
	Sep	95.83	-1.50%
	Oct	100.28	6.16%
	Nov	94.13	-4.20%
	Dec	87.59	-5.67%

Each annual return is calculated over 12 months.

On the face of it, it would seem that we have 12 times as many data points. The reasoning goes like this (I will refute these later on):

1. If we used non-overlapping data, we are essentially using only a December-to-December annual returns. By using overlapping monthly data, we have 12 times the accuracy.

2. Non-overlapping analysis is inefficient since it does not make use of all the available data.

3. Overlapping data avoids the issue of an arbitrary year end. Said differently, with non-overlapping data, why use December-to-December data? Perhaps this data masks a mid-year fall.

Despite these arguments for using overlapping data, the evidence still stacks against overlapping data.

The first and foremost argument against the use of overlapping data is that none of our statistical tests works on overlapping data. A basic assumption of statistical tests[65] is that the sample being tested represents *independent* experiments. Clearly, a January-to-January and the February-to-February return are not independent. They overlap by 11 months out of 12. Their correlation would be over 90%.[66] None of the results from statistical tests would be valid. The mathematics assumes (and requires) certain things to be true, one of which is independence. Without this, the calculations of goodness of fit, and the uncertainty (error estimate) or a parameter are simply not meaningful.

How important is independence? I give two examples.

I use a hypothetical example of a factory making widgets. Suppose you had a factory making a million widgets a month. Suppose your testing procedure made 100,000 tests and found no errors. This would be a comforting result. You cannot test each part, but testing 10% as a sample seems like an efficient way to go. Your factory seems to be likely turning out few or no defective widgets.

But wait. Suppose those 100,000 tests were all on the same widget. If you learned this, you probably would have less certainty that your factory was defect free. Admittedly, this is an extreme example. Let me change it. Suppose you actually tested 100,000 different widgets. Okay, we are comfortable again. Or are we? Suppose you have 12 factories and all the tests came from one factory. You could try to rationalize that the factories are identical or similar in an effort to reduce your *feeling* of uncertainty. In fact, if all the testing came from one of 12 factories, you would feel less certain of the result. The uncertainty in this example arose in both instances (the 1-widget-tested, and the 1-of-12-factors-tested) comes from the dependence in the sample. The samples are highly correlated, either reducing the certainty considerably, or wiping it out completely.

The second example is the presidential election of 1936 in the United States of America:

> "The 1936 campaign concluded with the Literary Digest … publishing survey results forecasting a landslide victory for the Republican presidential candidate,

Alf Landon. The incumbent, Franklin Roosevelt, by a large margin, of course, won the election. Thus the Literary Digest poll gained an infamous place in the history of survey research."[67]

The results were wrong because of sample dependence in the survey methodology.[68] It is possible to get a completely wrong answer when you fail to meet the assumptions required by the statistical tests you are using.

There is a method that has all the advantages that overlapping is usually accredited with (as stated above). However, it does not have the statistical drawbacks. It has an additional advantage of illustrating for management the uncertainty in the 1-in-200 year estimate.

Tip 78: Instead of using overlapping data, use several non-overlapping analyses and compare the results.

Instead of calculating the rolling average returns, Jan-to-Jan, Feb-to-Feb,..., Dec-to-Dec, and collecting them all into one big analysis, keep them in 12 separate analyses.

The following table illustrates the idea. We employ the same rolling annual returns from the overlapping analysis but rearrange them into 12 different series, according to the ending month. Each of the 12 series consists of non-overlapping returns.

In the table below, the long column of returns on the left represents the rolling, overlapping returns. These returns are rearranged in the table on the left into 12 different series of non-overlapping returns.

This produces 12 series (one is Jan-to-Jan, the next Feb-to-Feb, the last Dec-to-Dec) of non-overlapping annual returns. A separate analysis can be made on each return. Doing a separate analysis on 12 separate series is easy nowadays, given computing power. The fact that there are 12 series is no drawback at all.

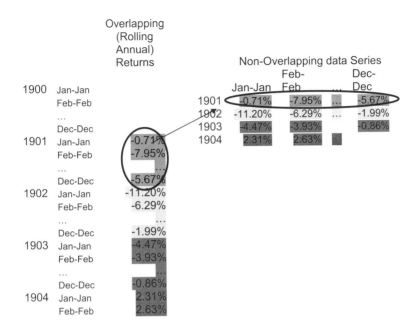

If we did 12 separate analyses on these series, this would address all of the alleged advantages of the overlapping analysis:

1. We have used the same number of data points with the 12 non-overlapping series that we would have with one, long, overlapping series. Using 12 non-overlapping series has the same number of data points as using one overlapping series.

2. This 12-series non-overlapping analysis uses all the available data and so is as efficient as the overlapping would have.

3. The 12-series non-overlapping analysis avoids the issue of an arbitrary year end.

Using the analysis with 12 non-overlapping series has an advantage over overlapping methodology.

4. The statistical tests work!

The assumptions of the statistics tests are not visibly violated with the 12-series non-overlapping approach.[69]

There is one other feature of the 12-non-overlapping series approach, which depending on your view is either an advantage or disadvantage. I view it as an advantage.

5. The 12 series may give different answers.
   a. This causes presentational issues.
   b. The final selection will require expert judgement.

One line of thinking says this is a disadvantage. "We need only one answer." "How do we know which is right?" This line of thinking would have us believe there is one absolute, preferably God-given, answer that is "correct." This view says there is no uncertainty in the answer. This is not my view.

My view is different. It is a central point of departure for the models discussed in this book. The different answers from the series illustrate the uncertainty in the results. This book views (and I view) this feature as a distinct advantage. Without this (or a similar) demonstration, there would be no evidence of uncertainty.

If I do not step on the scales in the morning, this does not prove I have no fat. Lack of evidence is not evidence of lack. Lack of evidence of fat is not evidence of lack of fat. Refusing to step on the scales in the morning is an example of an ostrich with its head in the sand. It is a fat ostrich. It indicates a lousy dieting strategy.

Similarly, lack of evidence of uncertainty is not evidence of lack of uncertainty. Different, equally plausible annual series (the 12 above) that give different answers forces us to come face to face with the true nature of the problem. Only once I step on the scales and see the weight of the issue (sorry for the pun) do I have a chance to start addressing the problem.

To remove any ambiguity, I emphasize that the 12 separate analyses must remain 12 separate analyses. Any attempt to combine them into one final answer appears to have the same drawbacks as using overlapping data. For example, after doing 12 analyses, you could develop 12 different distributions of annual returns. One idea (which is wrong) would be to then average the parameters from the 12 analyses to come up with one final answer. This solution appears to be as bad as using overlapping data.[70] This solution masks the uncertainty that 12 separate answers lays bare. As it turns out, there is no known way, to this author's knowledge, to combine these into a single answer.

Appendix 2: Basic Building Blocks

Capital models set capital by analysing potential losses from different possible events, and then the requiring capital to cover those future losses. For Solvency II the standard event is a 1-in-200 year event. What losses can occur once in every 200 years? The potential future loss over a 1-year horizon determines the amount of capital we must hold today.

The events that could occur are things such as equity markets falling precipitously, interest rates rising or falling, lapses increasing tremendously, policy continuation falling, excess claims, higher expenses, and so forth. We call these different risk factors.

To my knowledge, all players in the industry use two stages: analysing risks individually, and then in combination. The 1-in-200 loss from an individual risk analysis is known as a standalone loss or standalone capital requirement. The sum of all these is the undiversified capital.

When analysed in combination the 1-in-200 loss is called the diversified capital. The difference between these is the diversification benefit. Typically, the diversification benefit is the largest capital reduction for each insurer. I show examples of each of these later on in this appendix.

All Solvency II models follow a few basic steps:

Standalone risk factor analysis:

1. Determine all the risk factors of the model.
2. Model the individual risk factors on a standalone basis.
3. Figure out how the individual risk factors interact.

Aggregation:

4. Determine how the risk factors affect the eventual loss.
   a. Make a loss function of the risk factors.
5. Determine the aggregate loss and diversification benefit.
   (This is the point of this appendix.)
   a. Understand the uncertainty around this figure.
6. Understand what scenarios cause the aggregate loss.
7. Determine a distribution of the aggregate loss.

Follow-up:

8. Additional analysis, e.g. attribution of capital to risk or business unit.

Subject Matter Experts (SMEs) perform the standalone analysis. A mortality specialist would decide standalone models relating to mortality and longevity. Investment market experts would model equity falls, interest rate movements and currency movements, and so on. This book would be enormous if I tried to go into all the aspects relating to each individual risk factor, or potential risk factor. Fortunately, I do not need to. As discussed in Chapter 8, you have developed a team to address the specific needs for each area.

I do discuss aggregation. This is the subject of this appendix and the next. Aggregation is typically the most difficult aspect of a capital model. Your team should have a Subject Matter Expert just for aggregation. It is the place where the greatest gains in runs speeds and in understanding can be made.

This appendix introduces the basic methods of aggregation:

1. Correlation matrix aggregation
2. Monte Carlo aggregation
3. Targeted (or "Informed") Monte Carlo aggregation

The next appendix discusses mixing these basic methods into a staged aggregation.

I do not advocate using only one method for aggregation. This is in contrast with most industry participants that use only one method for the entire Solvency II model. A major distinguishing feature of this text is the modular approach in which different areas of the model use different aggregation methods. Each aggregation method provides different advantages and disadvantages, as becomes apparent below. By mixing and matching the aggregation models, we are able to tailor our model to be quick when possible and more detailed when necessary.

Before continuing, it is worth discussing in general terms what correlation matrix and Monte Carlo aggregations mean and to compare them with a couple of other terms you may have heard, in particular copula and scenario sampling.

As outlined above for the Solvency II model, when analysing, we identify the risk factors and decide a joint probability distribution for them. Technically, the distribution is usually a copula, though it might be an easy one, so easy that the word copula may not be used. Simple distributions are multivariate-Gaussian and Student-T distributions, though there are others. These are technically copulas, but you do not need to know that to use them.

Once we have decided the distribution for the risk factors, we may use any aggregation methodology. If we use an analytic formula, like a correlation matrix, to calculate the 1-in-200 year loss, we are using the distribution in a special way quickly to get an answer. We call this a closed-form solution for the 1-in-200 year loss. It is a simple formula, easy and quick to calculate.

Alternatively, we could sample many points. With this approach, we randomly select combinations of risk drivers in order to see the loss that occurs with each combination. Each combination of risk drivers is called a scenario and this process is called scenario sampling.

With both methods, we use the same assumption about the joint distribution of risk drivers. In this sense, the description of the joint distribution is separate and independent of the aggregation methodology. We could have a copula model that drives scenario sampling. We could have a copula model that is used in a correlation matrix approach. Likewise, a non-copula specification of a joint distribution of risk drivers could be used in either a correlation matrix or Monte Carlo approach.

With this in mind, let us continue with the different methodologies.

For purposes of this appendix, to display the basic methodologies, I use only two risk factors. This way, I can fit diagrams onto the page.

In this initial example, we model an overall portfolio of shares. Let us assume we have two sub-portfolios, A and B. You can think of them as being "local stocks" and "overseas stocks" if this helps. The idea is this: if we can analyse A and B separately, we can then combine (aggregate) these into an understanding of the overall portfolio.

Aggregation Step 1:

For Step 1 above, we must decide the risk factors.

> Let x be the return of portfolio A and
> Let y be the return of portfolio B.

Easy enough. Step 1 is always easy. It is just a list of the risk factors. (It may get more complicated when considering your strategy from
Chapter 4.)

Aggregation Step 2:

To do Step 2, we would analyse each risk factor separately. This is more involved. Typically, we gather historical data and analyse it statistically if possible. This would be natural for stocks, as in our example. Other risk factors may not have data and we might need to rely on expert judgement. Though we move through this step quickly here, in practice, this could be a lengthy step, especially since we must do it for each risk factor. This is where Subject Matter Experts perform their magic. A typical analysis might yield the following.

Risk Factor	Distribution	Mean	Standard Deviation
Return x	Normal	10%	21%
Return y	Normal	6%	18%

All the caveats regarding uncertainty from Chapter 6 come into play here. These parameters are not known with certainty. I discuss the effect of uncertainty below. It is significant. For this reason, I present the uncertainty (a 95% confidence interval) along with each risk factor. Remember that for Solvency II, for each estimate we make, we must present an indication of the uncertainty of it. I also include the 1-in-200 level for each distribution.

Risk Factor	Distribution	Mean	Standard Deviation	99.5% loss (using best estimate)
Return x	Normal	10% (7%-15%)	21% (15%-29%)	-44%
Return y	Normal	6% (2%-9%)	18% (12%-26%)	-40%

Aggregation Step 3:

For Step 3, we could decide that the correlation between x and y adequately describes the interaction between these two risk factors. This is an expert judgement, perhaps based on some analysis. I include an estimate of uncertainty. This usually requires a discussion between Subject Matter Experts of the related risks.

Correlation[71] between x and y	45% (30% - 60%)

I comment in passing that the confidence interval for our correlation estimate is narrower than typically found in practice.[72]

Steps 1 through 3 of an overall aggregation are generally similar for any aggregation methodology. Step 4, determining the loss function, demarks the point of divergence between all of the aggregation methodologies.

We first perform Steps 4 through 7 using a correlation matrix aggregation approach.

Correlation matrix approach:

Aggregation Step 4 (Correlation Matrix):

For Step 4, the loss of a stock portfolio is the size of the fund times the negative of the return. I suppose we have £600 of A and £400 of B.

$$Loss(x, y) = - [£600 \; x + £400 \; y]$$

Combining this with the information from the standalone 99.5% losses, we can calculate the standalone losses. For example, the Standalone loss for A is

$$Loss(\; x \; @ \; 99.5\%\text{-ile}, \; y \; @ \; 50\%\text{-ile}) = - \; [£600 \; (-44\%) + £400 \; (+6\%) \;] = £240$$

Please allow me a slight digression here to address a fine point. Some practitioners might find the above loss function surprising. The appearance of the 6% in the above formula may feel out of place. Some may feel we should use 0%. The alternate calculation is:

$$Loss(\; x \; @ \; 99.5\%\text{ile}, \; y = 0\%) = - \; [£600 \; (-44\%) + £400 \; (0\%) \;] = £264$$

The first answer assumes the mean of y to be the mean of the distribution, while the later assumes the mean to be zero. The former is more in keeping with Solvency II requirements that focus on losses over a 1-year horizon. In this definition, the mean over one year (in a real world sense) is not zero. It is whatever our analysis of historical returns indicates.

The later result, using the zero mean, may seem more natural for practitioners accustomed to using time-zero shocks, also known as instantaneous shocks. However, with a time-zero shock, there is no 1-year horizon over which to earn the median rate of 6%. This is why the 0% may seem more natural if you are used to doing time-zero shocks to determine capital. Notice, however, that using the 0% increases the loss by 24, from 240 to 264. This represents a 10% increase in capital for this example.

Tip 79: Using instantaneous (time-zero) stresses rather than a 1-year horizon can be expensive.

Use the non-zero (real world) mean for risk factors when describing the loss function.

I stress that using time-zero stresses <u>may</u> be expensive, but is not always so. It depends on other aspects of your model. When it is expensive, as a rule-of-thumb, by not using a 1-year horizon, you are giving up one year's return on your capital.

For example, if your capital earns 10% annually, then by using an instantaneous stress you would increase your capital requirement by 10%.[73] The reason for this is that over one year, before applying stresses, the assets will have earned one year of base-case returns and the liabilities will have provided one year of contributions to profit. This should be the company's return on capital. With this extra year of profits, there should be more room to buffer the effects of stresses.

Conceptually, we must distinguish between A) the return on assets backing capital, and B) the return on capital.

Return on Capital = Return on assets backing capital + profits from liabilities.

It is a common misconception to think that return on capital looks like an asset return. In fact, if an insurance company's capital were making a return like assets, why would we bother to have an insurance company? It is the extra profit that comes from the liabilities (and the assets backing them) that motivates owners of capital to invest in an insurance business.

There is a further technical point here. A company with more assets has higher capital requirements. To be absolutely clear on this, suppose you have two companies with identical liabilities (in size and type) and identical assets backing liabilities, and the same type of assets above liabilities. If one company has more assets above liabilities, that company will have a larger required capital. This is because the "delta-NAV" calculations used by Solvency II must be applied to the entire balance sheet. More assets mean more assets to stress. This results in a bigger change in assets and is a bigger capital requirement. Interestingly, you can avoid this extra charge with a one-year horizon by paying out the excess profits as a dividend. See Tip 11.

There are ways to mitigate this effect.[74] Tip 79 says that instantaneous shocks <u>can</u> be expensive but does not say that they always are. This tip is simply an indication that there is a material issue here and we need to address it. As a manager of insurance capital, do not increase capital simply by not using an instantaneous shock. A 1-year horizon can save a lot of capital. Alternatively, it is possible to adjust a zero stress to include the horizon mean, as done above.

Returning to the mainstream of the discussion, as stated above using

$$\text{Loss}(x, y) = - [\text{\pounds}600 \; x + \text{\pounds}400 \; y],$$

we get the standalone stresses at the 99.5% quantile of:

Standalone loss for A is
   Loss(x @ 99.5%-ile, y @ 50%-ile) = - [£600 (-44%) + £400 (+6%)] = £240

Standalone loss for B is

Loss(x @ 50%-ile, y @ 99.5%-ile) = - [£600 (+10%) + £400 (-40%)] = £100

Aggregation Step 5 (Correlation Matrix):

For Step 5, the correlation matrix uses the standalone 1-in-200 losses for the individual risk factors, along with the correlation to determine the aggregate loss.

Let L = vector of losses.
C = Matrix of correlations

Definition: Correlation Matrix Aggregate loss $= \sqrt{L^T C L}$

Diversification Benefit = (sum of standalone losses) - aggregate loss

In the example, $L = \begin{pmatrix} 240 \\ 100 \end{pmatrix}$ and $C = \begin{pmatrix} 1 & 0.45 \\ 0.45 & 1 \end{pmatrix}$. Then the aggregate loss (required capital) is calculated as:

$$= \sqrt{L^T C L}$$
$$= \sqrt{(240 \quad 100) \begin{bmatrix} 1 & .45 \\ .45 & 1 \end{bmatrix} \begin{pmatrix} 240 \\ 100 \end{pmatrix}}$$
$$= \sqrt{240^2 + 2 \times 0.45 \times (240)(100) + 100^2} = 299$$

In this case, we calculate the diversification benefit is (240+100) – 299 = 41.

It is worth noting the diversification benefit that we have seen in the above aggregate capital. While the 1-in-200 event for x (Sub-portfolio A) is a 44% loss, and for y (Sub-portfolio B) is a 40% loss, the aggregate loss is 30% (= 299 / 1000 with rounding). This is Tip 38 concerning diversification in action.

Many applications simply end here. The aggregate capital requirement of 299 and the diversification of 41 are "the answer(s)."

However, one point that we emphasize in this book is the uncertainty surrounding these figures. They above calculation arose from the best estimate of each parameter. Using the best estimate gave us an aggregate capital of 299.

However, if for the mean and standard deviation of x, instead of using the best estimates (10% and 21%) for both, we instead used the high end of the confidence intervals for both (15% and 29%) then the aggregate capital is 163.

Similarly, if we used the low end for mean and standard deviation of x (7% and 15%) then the aggregate capital is 449.

Here are a few calculation of capital, exploring some of the uncertainty in our parameters. Notice how much the required capital varies as we change the parameters used.

| Parameters | x | | | y | | | | |
	mean	standard deviation	1–in–200	mean	standard deviation	1–in–200	Correlation	Required Capital
Best Estimate	10%	21%	-44%	6%	18%	-40%	45%	299
x varies	15%	29%	-24%	6%	18%	-40%	45%	163
x varies	7%	15%	-68%	6%	18%	-40%	45%	449
y varies	10%	21%	-44%	9%	12%	-22%	45%	242
y varies	10%	21%	-44%	2%	26%	-65%	45%	390
Correlation varies	10%	21%	-44%	6%	18%	-40%	30%	288
Correlation varies	10%	21%	-44%	6%	18%	-40%	60%	312
All vary	15%	15%	-24%	9%	12%	-22%	30%	105
All-vary	7%	29%	-68%	2%	26%	-65%	60%	557

The capital could be from 105 to 557. That is a large range. This is Tip 43 in action.

We could pick a figure. Say the best estimate, or the highest or the lowest. This, however, is just a way to deny the uncertainty exists. Remember Tip 40: Fixing a parameter does not reduce its uncertainty.

We could attack the figures. For example, the 557 figure arises from the most extreme value of each parameter. "That does not seem likely," goes the refrain. There may be something to this if we think of the parameters as having a distribution. This says that the extremes are unlikely. If this line or reasoning seems plausible to you, you are likely a Bayesian at heart. (See Tip 45.)

However, for this exercise I showed a range for each parameter. These are ranges that we feel likely. They may not be confidence intervals, in the formal statistical sense. They just might be ranges we think could be possible. The ranges I presented are actually quite mild in comparison to those that arise in practice. Do you remember the discussion of the results of the Extreme Events Working Party after Tip 39?

In fact, there is no "solution" to uncertainty. Uncertainty is what remains after you have done all that you could. If you use sampling, there are calculation modifications you can do to reduce sampling error. When designing a survey or collecting data, there are things that you can do to reduce bias. Many professions, not just the actuarial one, have many ways of doing all that you can. However, all professions have limits. Okay, if you want I can say, "limits at the current time," leaving open the door to the notion that we might eventually conquer uncertainty. Nonetheless, once all the known and accepted avenues of thought have been explored, the remaining unknown part is uncertainty. We cannot "solve" it. We can only state it. Denying it would be wrong. (Also, not to acknowledge uncertainty is against professional standards, at least in the UK. See Endnote 46.)

When changing parameters more than one at a time, but still only one risk factor at a time, the lowest capital requirement is 163 and the highest is 449. The range for allowing all parameters to vary simultaneously is 105 to 557, as mentioned earlier. Notice that this range has a lower low and a higher high than the single-parameter-at-a-time version. The range for allowing only aggregation parameters to vary is 273 to 359.

The following table represents various measures of uncertainty.[75]

	Required Capital
Best Estimate	299
Range when Single Parameter varied one at a time	(214, 420)
Range when parameters of Single Risk Factor Varied	(163, 449)
Range when Aggregation Parameters Varied	(273, 359)
Range when All parameters Varied	(105, 557)

Table: Summary of Uncertainty of Capital Requirements.
Example of Portfolio with 2 sub-portfolios.

I mentioned earlier that the correlation matrix methodology (described above) has a copula version. Similar to the above, any elliptic distribution can be used to have a correlation-matrix-like solution.[76]

Aggregation Step 6 (Correlation Matrix):

With our aggregate loss (required capital) calculated, we can move on to Step 6: determining the scenarios that cause the loss. In our example, the loss is a simple function of the two risk factors, x and y, the returns of the two sub-portfolios. This loss function is linear. The graph below shows all combinations of x and y that provide the aggregate loss of 299.

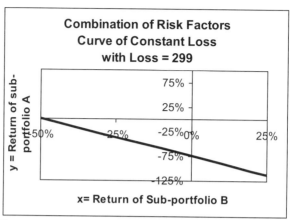

Figure: "Curve" (line) of Constant Loss for Loss = 299.
Loss(x, y) = - [£600 x + £400 y].

Any point along the line represents risk factors (x, y) that have a loss of 299.
This is the "line of constant loss." In general, the loss function may not be a line rather a curve, so we generally speak of a "Curve of Constant Loss."

Definition: A Curve of Constant Loss is a curve (graph) along which all points generate the same loss.

Tip 80: Know the Curve of Constant Loss.

The Curve of Constant Loss is essentially a contour of the loss function. The shape of it plays an important role in aggregation. How far the curve is from linear dictates the acceptability of using a correlation matrix approach.

This focus on the Curve of Constant Loss marks a distinct difference from some portions of the industry. Many speak of a "killer event," a single event that gives rise to the calculated aggregated loss. The above graph shows that there is not a single event, rather a line of points giving rise to the same loss. The Curve of Constant Loss is an entire contour of killer events. The view that there is a single killer event causes management to think too narrowly. Many practitioners know there are many killer scenarios but still choose to focus on only one.[77] This focus inappropriately narrows the view to only one possible disaster scenario, when in fact there are many we should consider.

The uncertainty from Step 5 affects the Curve of Constant Loss.

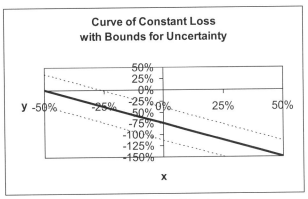

Figure: Bounds of Curve of Constant Loss.
Uncertainty represents range of capital requirements from varying all parameters of a single risk factor.

Aggregation Step 7 (Correlation Matrix):

In Step 7, we try to understand the distribution of the loss from the above overall analysis. In our particular example, x and y are Normal. Together they are multivariate Normal. The return on the final portfolio turns out also to be Normal, with mean 8.4% and standard deviation of 17.1%.[78]

This step of determining the distribution of the loss is not always performed in practice. Many practitioners calculate the loss, find a killer scenario and call it a day. However producing a distribution for the loss is crucial for our modular method. It is also good practice for understanding your model.

In the staged aggregation presented in the next appendix, the overall calculation is broken down into component aggregations. Each component is one in a series of aggregations. The next component requires not just a single number for the loss, but an entire distribution. While other methodologies may not have need of the distribution, in the staged methodology, it is crucial.

Fortunately, any aggregation methodology allows us to determine the loss distribution as required. This is true not only if the underlying distributions are Normal. It is true for functions that are more general. It is true for all elliptical functions, a class of functions that includes the popular Student-t distribution.[79]

Aggregation Step 8 (Correlation Matrix):

After aggregating capital, we perform other follow-up analysis. The primary example is attribution of capital back to business unit and back to risk factors. I do not focus on this step here since it is not important for the final capital number. I do discuss attribution in Tip 71: (Misc.) Use Negative Capital Attribution.

Monte Carlo Approach:

We now redo the analysis using a Monte Carlo approach. This means that we do not use a simple formula for aggregation. The correlation matrix approach used the correlation matrix to combine the effect of individual risk stresses. In Monte Carlo, we use random sampling of risk driver combinations and witness the result of many combinations. With enough scenarios tested, we can estimate the 1-in-200 year event without making assumptions about the aggregation. We do need to make assumptions about how to perform sampling. We also need to know how many samples to try. As we see later on, these aspects of Monte Carlo limit the reliability of the results.

As discussed above, the outline of the analysis uses the same 8 steps. The first 3 steps are the same as the correlation matrix approach. Using the same example as before, we continue on to Step 4 of the process.

The Monte Carlo method provides a way to handle assumptions that are more difficult. In particular, it allows non-linear loss functions. There is a computational cost. Unlike the correlation matrix approach that allows a single expression to calculate the aggregate required capital, the Monte Carlo approach allows no (closed-form) solution. Instead, Monte Carlo tests a number of combinations of risk factors, witnesses their loss, and determines from this sample what the 1-in-200 loss must be.

A small set-up might test 1,000 scenarios. Then the scenario with the 5th largest loss would be an estimate of a 1-in-200 event. (Some practitioners use the 6th largest loss.)

In the above small example, the fact that the final analysis depends on the results of a hand full of scenarios causes simulation error. Scenario simulation involves random sampling. Accordingly, the 5th scenario has a random element to it. This usually justifies doing a large number of simulations, more like 100,000, or if possible 1,000,000.

To illustrate this, we redo the previous example from the Correlation Matrix example using a Monte Carlo Approach.

Aggregation Step 4 (Monte Carlo):

To juxtapose the previous approach, I chose a lognormal model for equity returns. This is a standard assumption. It forms the basis of the Black-Scholes option pricing formula and many other models, for one thing. For these variables, we have to reinterpret the individual risk factors. (This is a slight back track to Step 2.)

To maintain some level of comparability, I will have the standalone 1-in-200 loss be the same for sub-portfolios A and B, -44% and -40% respectively, expressed in simple returns.[80] I also maintain the same means.[81] The adjusted parameters are as follows:

Risk Factor	Distribution	Mean	Standard Deviation	99.5% loss (using best estimate)
Log-Return x	Normal	9.5% (6.8%-14.0%)	26.2% (17.1%-44.6%)	-44%
Log-Return y	Normal	5.8% (2.0%-8.6%)	22.1% (14.9%-46.7%)	-40%
Correlation between x and y	45% (30% - 60%)			

With this reinterpretation of Step 2 complete, we assume the same correlation between the risk factors to complete Step 3.

Now we may perform Step 4 of the process: specifying the loss as a function of the risk factors:

$$Loss(x, y) = - [\pounds600 (e^x - 1) + \pounds400 (e^y - 1)]$$

Aggregation Step 5 (Monte Carlo):

With that done, we move onto Step 5: determining the aggregate loss and the diversification benefit.

With the above set-up, after running 1,000 scenarios, noting the 5th largest loss, we obtain a capital requirement of 289. This compares with the 299 in the correlation matrix approach. However, this figure depends on the choice of 1,000 random scenarios. It could change with new runs. To understand this potential simulation error, we rerun the analysis. Each of the following figures represents the 5th worst loss from a new run of 1,000 scenarios:

289 (the above figure), 297, 314, 305, 291, 291, 295, 309, 269, 280

The above 10 capital estimates came from 10,000 simulations in total. There are 10 estimates. Each estimate is the 5th worst from 1,000 simulations.[82]

135

This is a large range, from a low of 269 to a high of 314. The average of these 10 estimates is 294 and the standard deviation is 13.4. This is a range of 17%. Many would view this as a wide range and would say it is unacceptable. There is a lot of uncertainty surrounding the capital estimate.

The standard solution is to use more simulations. Rather than calculating the capital requirement from 1000 simulations, we could use 10,000. Performing this analysis 10 times (for 100,000 simulations), we obtain the following 10 capital requirement estimates:

290, 292, 296, 298, 293, 296, 286, 290, 298, and 288.

The above 10 capital estimates came from 100,000 simulations. Each estimate is the 50th worst from 10,000 simulations.

These runs range from 286 to 298 with a percentage range of about 4%. This range of estimates is narrower than the previous 10 simulations. By moving from 1,000 simulations per estimate to 10,000 simulations per estimate, our uncertainty has been reduced, from a range that was 14-17% wide to one that is about 4% wide. However, this increase in accuracy came at a steep price: we had to run 10 times as many scenarios. Further reduction in the estimate would require another multiplier to the effort. In practice, a 4% simulation error could be accepted for reasons of practicality.

When using a Monte Carlo aggregation, the designer would explore the number of scenarios to use only once. This would be when building the Internal Model. For example, during the process of building the model, a practitioner might do the above analysis with 100,000 scenarios, taken 10 times at 10,000 per run. After viewing the results, she might decide that 10,000 simulations are enough for future runs of the model. After that decision, no future runs would test 100,000. Instead, they would do the less time intensive 10,000. I say 10,000 not because this is a magic number nor one particularly used in practice. I use 10,000 just to be consistent with my above example. In practice, the decision is often a much higher number.[83]

I chose one of the 10 runs of 10,000 to continue with this example. The aggregate loss (required capital) for this set of runs is 292. Accordingly, we can calculate the diversification benefit as:

Diversification benefit   = sum of standalone losses − aggregate capital
                        = (240+100) − 292 = 48.[84]

This compares to the Correlation Matrix example's aggregated capital of 299 and diversification benefit of 41. It may not always be the case that the Monte Carlo method provides a lower (higher) aggregate capital (diversification benefit) than then Correlation matrix approach.

Aggregation Step 6 (Monte Carlo):

Step 6 of our 8-step method is to understand what scenarios cause the aggregate loss. In the Monte Carlo approach, we do this my examining the simulations to determine which ones provide a loss similar to the final aggregate loss. The 10,000 simulations are ordered according to the final loss value. We had to do this to determine the 50th largest loss. We consider the losses above and below this loss value. The table below shows a portion of this ordered list. It includes the 50th largest loss simulations (the one used to set the aggregate loss) and the 10 simulations above and below this on the ordered list.

Position in Ordered List	Simulated Loss	Sub-port A's return		Sub-port B's return	
		Log-return	Simple Return	Log-return	Simple Return
60	283	-0.435	-0.196	-35.3%	-17.8%
59	284	-0.418	-0.219	-34.2%	-19.7%
58	285	-0.407	-0.236	-33.4%	-21.0%
57	285	-0.293	-0.402	-25.4%	-33.1%
56	285	-0.272	-0.437	-23.8%	-35.4%
55	285	-0.461	-0.172	-37.0%	-15.8%
54	285	-0.426	-0.213	-34.7%	-19.2%
53	288	-0.473	-0.168	-37.7%	-15.5%
52	290	-0.371	-0.302	-31.0%	-26.1%
51	290	-0.276	-0.453	-24.1%	-36.4%
50	**292**	**-0.338**	**-0.356**	**-28.6%**	**-30.0%**
49	294	-0.411	-0.260	-33.7%	-22.9%
48	294	-0.286	-0.448	-24.9%	-36.1%
47	294	-0.466	-0.194	-37.2%	-17.7%
46	295	-0.341	-0.361	-28.9%	-30.3%
45	295	-0.414	-0.260	-33.9%	-22.9%
44	296	-0.262	-0.502	-23.0%	-39.4%
43	299	-0.404	-0.287	-33.3%	-24.9%
42	300	-0.433	-0.252	-35.1%	-22.2%
41	300	-0.426	-0.260	-34.7%	-22.9%
40	301	-0.455	-0.228	-36.6%	-20.4%

To illustrate the relationship between the risk factors that give rise to the aggregate loss, the following figure graphs the above aggregate loss and the 10 points on either side. We have estimated the Curve of Constant Loss from this.[85] Notice that the Curve of Constant Loss appears linear.

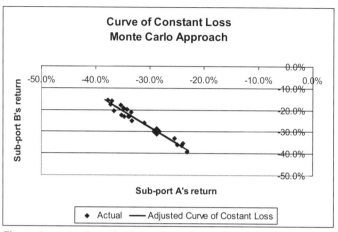

Figure: Aggregate Loss simulation (large diamond) and simulations with 10 nearest greater losses and 10 nearest lower losses.

Tip 81: Linear loss functions often suffice. This is triply true when we are honest about parameter uncertainty.

We return to the issue that the Curve of Constant Loss appears linear in our Monte Carlo estimates in the next appendix. For now, it is sufficient to say that we understand which scenarios in our Monte Carlo analysis give rise to a Curve on Constant Loss on which the loss is the aggregate loss.

Aggregation Step 7 (Monte Carlo):

Our next step of the aggregation process is to determine the distribution of the aggregate loss. Rather than estimating the 1-in-200 loss, we seek the distribution of the loss for any quantile. This is easy or hard, depending on your point of view.

The easy view says, "We have 10,000 points estimating the loss. This forms an empirical distribution." The following graph shows the cumulative distribution of losses from the empirical distribution of the 10,000 simulated losses.

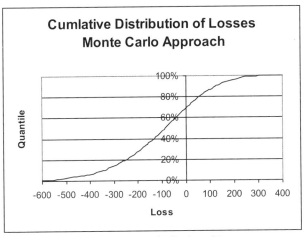

Figure: Cumulative Distribution of Losses
From 10,000 Monte Carlo (Lognormal) Simulations

The harder view says, "We do not know a formula for this distribution. Is it Normal, Student-T, or something else?" One solution is to run statistical tests on the 10,000 points in hope of finding an analytic distribution that fits the Monte Carlo simulations. With this approach, a good fit is invariably hard to find. The statistical tests are too demanding for 10,000 points.[86]

The thing to do in this case is remember the uncertainty in the parameters. When we consider this, the Normal distribution usually suffices as a good fit.

Tip 82: The Normal distribution suffices when uncertainty is considered.

When fitting distributions to simulated date, we must account for the parameter uncertainty in the simulation.

For our example, I varied the means and standard deviation parameters of our sub-portfolio returns along with their correlation parameter. While doing this, it is important to keep each parameter within its range of acceptable values. This changes the loss distribution. From the different combinations of parameters, we can form a highest and a lowest distribution. Any fitted distribution should lie between these bounds. The result for our example is in the following graph.

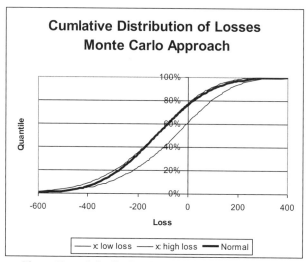

Figure: Normal distribution fits (mostly) within bounds
arising from parameter uncertainty

The Normal distribution shown above fits between the low and high bounds for distributions when considering the uncertainty of the parameters. This means we can use the Normal distributions as an approximate loss function. When we are honest about the uncertainty in our original parameters, our life is easier.

Some practitioners may get concerned that the Normal distribution hugs one bound in the tails and another in the body of the distribution.[87] There is no clear principle to reject the Normal distribution on these grounds, however. By using the Normal distribution, we save a lot of time in running the model. It is practical to use a fitted distribution that fits within the high and low bounds.

Aggregation Step 8 (Monte Carlo):

As before, there are follow-up steps to do after the aggregation, in particular attribution. As before, I do not go into attribution here since it does not affect the aggregate capital number. See Tip 71: (Misc.) Use Negative Capital Attribution

Targeted Monte Carlo Aggregation:

Our last aggregation is a variant on the previous methodology. To motivate the idea, we look at a typical Monte Carlo analysis in which most of the points tested are performed away from the Curve of Constant Loss. The following figure illustrates this. The data used comes from our above example.

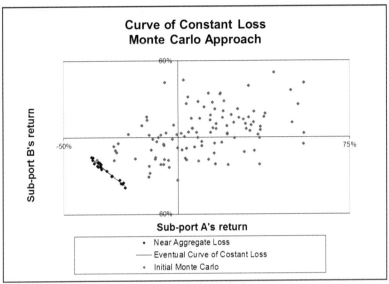

Figure: Standard (Shotgun) Monte Carlo Analysis
Many samples are made from the loss function. The samples are chosen by using the (joint) distribution of the risk factors. Most sampled points are away from the Curve of Constant Loss.

It would be more efficient if we could test points near the Curve of Constant Loss. Before we begin, however, we may not know where the Curve of Constant Loss is. How can we focus our Monte Carlo testing there?

I refer to the standard Monte Carlo method as "shotgun" because it shoots all at once. We select each scenario with the same probability as any other. No information from earlier scenario tests is used to "aim" the later scenario tests.

Targeted Monte Carlo begins by performing a relatively low number of simulations. This low number is used to form an initial estimate of the Curve of Constant Loss. We use fewer sample points but still enough to get an estimate of the Curve of Constant Loss.

Tip 83: Targeted Monte Carlo speeds up Monte Carlo.

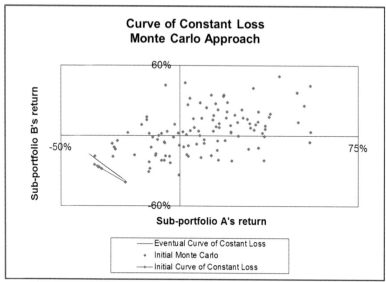

Figure: Targeted Monte Carlo Analysis, Initial Sample.
Fewer samples are tried than the Shotgun Monte Carlo. Enough are used to make
a rough estimate of the Curve of Constant Loss.

The number of points near the Curve of Constant Loss is in the same proportion as in a
shotgun approach. Only the absolute number is lower since there are fewer scenarios.[88]

In this first stage of targeted Monte Carlo, we have not used our entire scenario testing
capability, only a small portion of it. Perhaps we use between 1% and 10% of our entire
capability. This gives us plenty of run capability (ammunition) to do more targeted
analysis.

The next figure includes all the points from the above the initial sample, plus the sampled
points of the next samples, the targeted simulations.

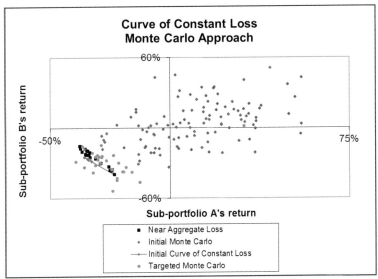

Figure: Targeted Monte Carlo Analysis, Initial & Next Samples
The initially sample points are in red. These result in the Curve of Constant Loss
in purple. The newly sampled points are in green. The new points explore the
area around the initially estimated Curve of Constant Loss.

The distribution used to sample the scenarios around the initial Curve of Constant Loss is
different from the underlying distribution of the risk drivers. We have to develop a
separate distribution for sampling that is different from the distribution of the underlying
risk factors.

In one dimension, this would look like the following figure. Here, we shift the actual
distribution so that the sampling distribution has a mean that is at the 1-in-200 level of the
actual distribution.

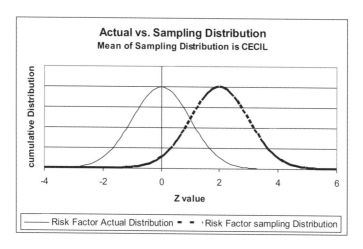

Actual vs. Sampling Distribution
Mean of Sampling Distribution is CECIL

Risk Factor Actual Distribution ▬ ▬ ▪Risk Factor sampling Distribution

In higher dimensions, we would make the translation from the actual distribution to the Curve of Constant Loss. The sampling distribution would travel along the ray (arrow) from base case to a particular point along the Curve of Constant Loss.

Some technical considerations arise when changing the sampling distribution to be centred on the Curve of Constant Loss. The change is a direct process.[89]

The advantage of targeted Monte Carlo is that it is more efficient. We use a few simulations to get a rough approximation of an initial Curve of Constant Loss. We continue simulating losses, but only a few at a time. After each portion of simulation, we refine our estimate of the Curve of Constant Loss before proceeding. When our estimate of the Curve of Constant Loss appears stable, we can cease simulating losses. We are done.

Appendix 3: Staging the Analysis

The phrase "divide and conquer" characterizes the modular approach advocated here. In this appendix, the overall capital model will be broken down into smaller components allowing experts in certain areas to focus on a specific component. This speeds up the entire process tremendously. It also makes the model used more, supporting further innovation with the models. Most importantly, the subdivision makes an understandable model.

When calculating capital, there is an ordering to the component aggregations. Results from lower level aggregations feed upward into higher level ones. This process continues until we reach the top aggregation. The top aggregation provides the final aggregated capital.

This mix-and-match aspect of staging provides a crucial component for fulfilling many other goals mentioned in this book. By subdividing risk, we can:

- Make components for different decision makers:

    o Tip 29: Know who make decisions about product allocations.
    o Tip 53: Structure your model-creation team as a fluid pyramid.
    o Tip 56: Make sure any (and all) decision makers necessary for sign-off are in the 2nd layer of the pyramid.[90]

- The model runs quickly:

    o Tip 47: Models must run quickly.
    o Models can include risk factors that are more detailed. (See end of this appendix.)

- Usability enhanced.

- Intuition enhanced:

    o Tip 48: Design your models and processes to build intuition.

- Structure relates to actionable decisions:

    o All of **Chapter 3**.

- Supports the Use Test for Solvency II Internal Model application.

- The speed that these models run allows us to incorporate more desirable model elements. See discussion below.

Armed with the basic aggregation methods from the previous appendix, we are set to develop your overall capital model. This appendix motivates and illustrates the modular methodology that I advocate.

I start by motivating the modular approach by discussing the limitations of the basic aggregations models.

Limitation 1: The huge correlation matrix.

When used for an entire aggregation model, both the correlation matrix and the Monte Carlo aggregation approaches employ a large correlation matrix. The former obviously does. The latter uses it as the simulation engine for determining scenarios in which to calculate losses.

In either approach, the number of correlation terms grows quickly with the number of risk factors. This can be seen in the following table:

Number of Risk Factors	Number of correlations
2	1
3	3
10	45
20	190
30	435

The number of correlation parameters grows with the square of the number of risk factors.[91]

Estimating all those correlations is hard.[92] With more risk factors, estimation of the correlations becomes more difficult. One reason is the sheer number of correlation parameters, obviously.

Another difficulty is the esoteric nature of some of the correlations. For example, our interest rate model might have several factors for interest rates (level, steepness, etc.). This is typical. Our mortality model might also have several parameters, such as a pandemic mortality risk factor (among others). We would need to develop a correlation between pandemic mortality and interest rate steeping risk factors, for instance. In another portion of the correlation matrix, we must also develop correlations between earthquake and property level risk factors, or between mass lapse and real yields. I think you get the idea.

These correlations usually have few historic data points. Accordingly, the uncertainty (confidence interval) of these correlation estimates would be huge. Alternatively, setting these correlations by expert judgement would still involve considerable uncertainty. Remember Tip 40: Fixing a parameter does not reduce its uncertainty.

The correlations have a large impact.

With a large number of such correlations, we may choose to make several correlations equal to 0%. Alternatively, we might be conservative and make them 25%, which would have a material impact (potentially) when done with a large number of correlations.

Remember Tip 43: Aggregation carries or amplifies uncertainty.

Also, recall Tip 44: Know that the uncertainty of correlations is enormous. This has large effects on the final required capital.

Limitation 2: Linear loss is not always a good estimate.

I would like to provide a prototypical non-linear loss model. This example behaves sufficiently badly that it simply does not fit in any way into a linear loss model. This provides a clear example, a proto-typical example, for when Monte Carlo is necessary.

For illustration, I chose an operational risk example. Suppose our operational risk has two risk factors. Suppose each has a chance of being zero loss. Say these two probabilities are 60% and 30%. When not zero, the loss severity is 1,000 times a log variable. I assume the correlation between the risk factors is zero.[93]

It is possible to confuse this model with a linear model because it is the sum of two losses. However, the factors themselves are not Normal, not even Lognormal. Each factor is a mixed Binomial-Lognormal distribution. This means that it is not possible to make the final combined loss into a linear model either of z-scores or of other elliptic random variables.

Below I graph the Curve of Constant Loss of the 1-in-200 loss. Notice that this Curve of Constant Loss is a right angle with a rounded corner. This is about as far away from a straight line as you can get.

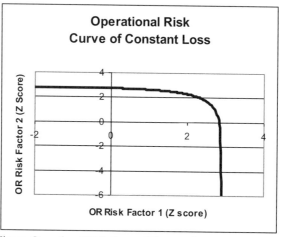

Figure: Operational Risk Curve of Constant Loss

Any effort to approximate this curve with a linear assumption leads to bad results. In this situation, we must employ a Monte Carlo aggregation.[94]

Not only would a correlation matrix approach (with its linear assumption) provide a poor estimate, to this curve. It would provide a capital requirement that is <u>lower</u> than an exact calculation. The correlation matrix is less conservative. This places the linear approximation in violation of the regulations requiring that any method be at least as stringent as an accurate calculation would be. This is further reason to use a Monte Carlo aggregation in this situation.

There is no doubt that this operational risk loss would need to be done via a Monte Carlo aggregation approach. The loss function permits no other option.

As I said at the beginning of Limitation 2, this is a prototypical case in which linear loss does not work well. Not all cases work this poorly. There may be similar models with mixed distributions that could be approximated by linear loss functions usefully. The point here is only that linear loss can fail dramatically.

<u>Limitation 3</u>: Formula-fitted loss functions.

Estimating the loss for any simulation can be intensive. This is in contrast to the examples given in the previous appendix. There, I defined a short formula that calculated the loss for any risk factors. In practice, the calculation of loss involves much more complex, involved calculations.

It may be that even a large insurer might find it difficult to calculate 200 or 300 loss values in a financial quarter. Compare this with a Monte Carlo aggregation approach for which 10,000 simulations would appear to be a low number for getting a good estimate. Industry participants generally required at least 100,000 simulations and arguments for more are common.

There are many actuarial valuation systems. I do not want to list all systems available for purchase, partly because it is not my goal to endorse any particular system here, and partly because you may be using an internal system. I am sure you are aware, however that there are complicated actuarial systems. Often, there are different systems for different products. This adds the complication of tying all the results together into an overall result. (Remember, I use the word "Model" to be the sum of all subsystems, their interfaces and the decision processes surrounding these.)

The most common method for addressing this issue is to create a "formula-fitted loss function." Essentially, this takes a few complicated runs, and makes a simple function out of them that can be used more widely. We run a number of valuations in the actuarial systems, a number like 200-300. These are sometime called "slow runs," "detailed valuations," "heavy lifts," or similar phrases to capture the laborious and time-consuming nature of these calculations. I use the term "heavy lifts." The results of the heavy lifts form the basis of a simple loss function, like the one we used in the last appendix. This simple loss function is the formula-fitted loss function. This loss function is quick to use. In a Monte Carlo approach, we use the formula-fitted function for the large number of simulations.

Both Monte Carlo and correlation matrix approaches use heavy lifts to calculate the standalone losses for each risk driver. From there, we find a killer scenario. (Recall that most implementations focus on only one killer scenario, unlike the method presented here that tries to find the Curve of Constant Loss.)

Monte Carlo uses the formula-fitted loss function in a large number of scenarios to do this while the correlation matrix approach finds a point analytically under the assumption of linear loss. Both methods admit that the loss may not be accurate. After aggregation, we perform another heavy lift to "true-up" the loss value.[95]

The issues surrounding formula-fitting are so large that I dedicate a separate appendix to their discussion, Appendix 4: Only as Good as your Loss Function. It suffices to say here that this may be the weak link in the aggregation chain, for both Monte Carlo and correlation matrix aggregation approaches.

Limitation 4: One size does not fit all.

If one of the basic aggregation methods were used for the entire model then we are at a disadvantage. If the entire model is one large Monte Carlo simulation, all risks run slowly. This includes the easier risks that we could have approximated well with a linear model. Alternatively, if an overall correlation matrix method is employed then particularly nonlinear risk interaction will be poorly estimated.

Limitations 1 through 4 represent the difficulties when we use basic aggregation (from the previous appendix) as a big aggregation of everything. We cannot use a slow model for tactical decisions, and neither can we use an inaccurate one. This leads to a Deathstar system which is slow, difficult to develop, resource intensive to maintain and provides little or no timely management information with which to manage the business day to day. (See all the tips from Tip 46 to Tip 51.)

Tip 84: Use staged aggregation. (correlation matrix approach)

I advocate a modular approach to aggregation. The overall aggregation is broken down into stages. The aggregation model at each stage is called a component or a module. The terms are interchangeable.

If you have any background in Solvency II, you already know a staged methodology. The Standard Formula for Solvency II employs a staged aggregation methodology. Rather than having one big correlation matrix, the problem is broken down into stages. Each component of the Standard Formula employs a correlation matrix aggregation approach. I outline this approach below. Along the way, we can see that this staged methodology addresses Limitations 1 directly.

Quantitative Impact Study 5 (QIS 5) used this methodology. QIS 5 was an industry-wide test-run for the new capital requirement calculations. I include the staging (hierarchy) from QIS 5 as a sample. The Standard Formula of Solvency II uses a similar methodology.

In QIS 5, the overall Solvency Capital Requirement (SCR) is staged in to Basic SCR, Operational Risk and Adjustments. Of these, only the Basic SCR is supported by further analysis. In the staging terminology, we refer to this as the first stage.

Basic SCR is broken down into Market, Health, Default, Life, Non-life and Intangibles. These are broad risk classes. They represent the second stage.

Default and Intangibles have no lower sub-stages, but all of the other second stage risk classes do. For example, Market is broken down into Interest-Rate risk, Equity, and so on. These represent the third stage.

There is a fourth stage. Some fourth stage elements are in the diagram. For example, Non-SLT Health from the third stage has lower stages Premium Received and Lapse. In practice, there may be elements used during the QIS 5 that do not appear on the diagram. For example, practitioners typically treat interest rates via a principle component analysis (PCA) that breaks the yield curve into (typically) 3 components: PCA1, PCA2 and

PCA3. This essentially provides and additional fourth stage under the Interest Rate Risk (which is third stage).

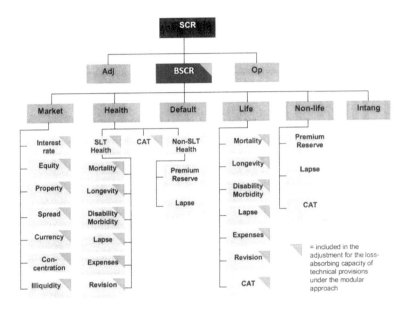

Diagram[96]: from QIS 5 showing an early version of modular design.

The above is a particular staging arrangement to use in an overall correlation matrix approach. Other arrangements are possible.

With the above staging, we must decide exactly how to derive the capital. At the highest level, we calculate the Basis SCR with the following formula:

$$\text{Basic SCR} = \sqrt{\sum Cor_{i,j} \times SCR_i \times SCR_j}$$

Here, SCR_i is the standalone 99.5% loss for the risk class i, and $Cor_{i,j}$ is the correlation between classes i and j. So, there are SCR_{Market}, SCR_{Health}, $SCR_{Default}$, SCR_{Life}, $SCR_{Non-Life}$ and $SCR_{Intangibles}$. For QIS 5, the regulator specified the related correlations. In an Internal Model, they are set by judgement or historical analysis.

Sub-stages have sub-correlations matrices. For example,

151

$$\text{SCR}_{\text{Market}} = \sqrt{\sum Cor_{u,v} \times SCR_u \times SCR_v}$$

Here, SCR_u is the standalone 99.5% loss for the risk factor u, where u runs through the Market risk factors: Interest Rate, Equity, Property, etc. Each sub-stage has a related module with its own correlation matrix. In the pure staged correlation matrix approach, each sub-stage performs the aggregation using a correlation matrix as above.

The above illustrates that overall aggregation is staged into a type of pyramid. Each upper level stage requires SCR estimates from the lower stages immediately below. As we look lower down the staging, we eventually end in a risk factor that has no lower stages.

The correlations are provided in a separate correlations matrix.[97] The individual SCRs are calculated for each sub-module. Each sub-module in turn may have sub-sub- and so forth, for as many stages as necessary.

I comment in passing that the big correlation approach and the staged correlation approach are not equivalent. There is a common misconception that a staged correlation matrix approach and a one-large-correlation-matrix approach are equivalent.[98]

This approach allows the company (and the regulators and outside investors) to focus on the important correlations without getting bogged down on the unimportant (read not materially large) ones.[99]

1. There are fewer parameters to look at, which aides understanding considerably.

2. The staging of risk factors naturally coincides with the level of detail needed for different levels of manager. A high-level manager can get the overview by looking at the list of risk modules overall correlation matrix for these.

3. Down the management chain, the list of sub-modules and the correlation matrix for each informs those managers of each of those sub-risk factors. Each detail is minded by an appropriately focused Subject Matter Expert.

To elaborate on this last point, each high level manager would look at his broad risk classes. The overall life actuary would be looking at one set of risk factors, such as mortality, longevity, lapse, etc., and their correlations. The overall non-life actuary would be looking at a different set of risk factors, such as mortality premium & reserve, catastrophe, lapse, etc., and their correlations. The Chief Investment Officer would look at yet another set of sub-risk factors, such as interest rate risk, equity risk, currency, etc., and their correlations. And so forth.

Below these high level managers would be colleagues looking at the sub-sub-risk factors. For example, the longevity analyst might have different factors for longevity, like overall level and trend. These sub-sub-risk factors would have their own correlations. In another portion of the organization, under the investment manager, an interest rate expert separates yield curve movement into principle components. For each stage and each branch dividing the risk factors, there would be a separate analysis of risk factors and correlation matrix.

I have described this staging from top to bottom. To calculate capital, however, we proceed from bottom to top. The lowest level components are calculated first. Each risk factor gives rise to a 99.5% loss. The lowest component aggregation aggregated these risks. The result is a 99.5% loss for that component. This result is passed up to the next higher level module where it is used as a risk factor. That in turn is aggregated and the result passed upward. Eventually, we reach the top of the hierarchy. The result there the overall aggregated (Basic) Solvency Capital Requirement.

When designing the staged aggregation, every time we introduce a new sub-module, it is necessary to provide a correlation matrix in order to specify how to aggregate to the upper module. Even though this introduces more matrices, the use of staging greatly reduces the total number of correlation parameters. Even three stages can reduce the number of correlation parameters by a factor of 10.[100]

Tip 85: Staged aggregation dramatically reduces the number of correlation parameters.

The above staging of risk factors greatly reduces the number of correlations parameters. This mitigates the Limitation 1 concerning the number of parameters and their estimation. We can tailor the number and structure of parameters to the management structure of the company and the focus of the organization. We can get rid of parameters we do not need while keeping those that we do.

Tip 86: Place in one staged component, all risk factors that interact directly.

I mention that one criticism of the Standard Formula does not apply to staged aggregation in general. Many practitioners complain that the Standard Formula does not allow for proper interaction of certain risks. For example, lapse risk is in the life insurance model but it may relate to market risks, such as equity market returns or bond yields. The Standard Formula only crudely accounts for this relationship via a single correlation between insurance risks and market risks. Most practitioners feel that this treatment accounts poorly for the relationship between lapse and market returns for those products that are rate sensitive. They are right.

This criticism of the Standard Formula is a criticism of a particular staging hierarchy, not all staging methods in general. Other staging aggregations can place lapse and market risk factor in the same component. This allows us to employ a more dynamic relationship, one that more satisfactorily captures the relationship between these risks. The trick is to arrange your risks so that strongly related risks are in the same component.

The proper staging to use differs from company to company.

For example, with some products (e.g. with-profits products in the UK) the overall portfolio return drives the policyholder behaviour, not the individual returns of equity, bonds or property. This leads to a potential requirement for our staging for a staging component above market returns that creates portfolio returns, specifically to use in any lapse or persistency models.

The difficulty, which is mentioned again in Tip 100, is that different products may require different risk factors to be grouped into components together. How to address this problem will vary form company to company.

Tip 87: Use staged aggregation. (Monte Carlo approach)

Staging the aggregation strengthens not only a pure correlation matrix approach. It also strengthens the Monte Carlo approaches as well.

Not all of the components in our staging have to be correlation matrix aggregation. One or more of the components can employ a Monte Carlo aggregation.

The requirements for a Monte Carlo aggregation are more demanding. It is not enough to have only 99.5% losses for each risk factor, as in the correlation matrix aggregation. Monte Carlo requires an entire distribution for each risk factor. However, this is available. Step 7 in the aggregation methodology used in Appendix 2 calculates the distribution of losses for an aggregation. If one component uses Monte Carlo aggregation, the components below it provide the entire distribution of losses, as needed.

An additional requirement from a Monte Carlo component would be the interactions between risk factors, e.g. the correlations. However, this interaction is set outside of the aggregation methodology, independent of the component. Such a requirement is not passed up the hierarchy in a staged aggregation. Accordingly, this requirement for Monte Carlo is also met. Even though the requirements for a Monte Carlo aggregation are more demanding, they are met in a staged aggregation methodology.

The advantages of a staged approach concerning Limitation 1 (Huge correlation matrix) above apply to Monte Carlo aggregations as well as they do for correlation matrix approaches. Most Monte Carlo simulations use a correlation matrix at the core of the scenario generator. Just as before, these require understanding and calibrating. The savings in the overall number of these correlation parameters applies.

There is a methodology for handling many risk factors that breaks them down into small groups of risk factors at a time, even as few as 2-at-a-time. The methodology utilizes pair-copulas.[101] We can use the same staging structure described above for the correlation matrix approach. A staging structure using pair-copulas is referred to as a "vine" because the diagram resembles a vine, with branches connecting risk factor clusters.

The point here is that the same reduction in correlation parameters that we achieved via staging in the correlation matrix approach is also achievable in a Monte Carlo approach. By arranging the correlation matrices in stages, we can greatly reduce the number of correlation parameters necessary to describe our interdependence. This works for both Monte Carlo and correlation matrix approaches.

Tip 88: Staging allows different aggregation methods for different parts of our overall model.

This tip indicates the main benefit of staging. We can mix and match aggregation methodologies to allow for fast and accurate aggregation.

Staging provides more benefits than simply fewer correlation parameters. By staging our risk factors, we may alter the model used at each stage. We may employ Monte Carlo where best, a correlation matrix approach where that is best.[102]

Tip 89: In a staged aggregation, choose each module to be Correlation Matrix if it can be, Monte Carlo if it must be.

The reason for preferring a correlation matrix approach is speed. With a fast model, managers can use it on a daily basis. We can rerun the model if there is a problem. More importantly, we can rerun simply in order to test out new scenarios and sensitivities of results. In this manner, users gain intuition about models that run fast because they see it in action so many times. They rely on it more. They give more feedback how to improve it, making a positive spiral of use-improve-trust-use. I have expounded on this feature of models earlier when disparaging Deathstar systems. A staged aggregation with correlation matrix modules fulfils these requirements.

Tip 82 described that when fitting a distribution, we must account for parameter uncertainty. When uncertainty is included in our models honestly, then usually a normal (or other elliptic) distribution can be used for the loss distribution.

Tip 81 also indicated that linear loss functions are often an acceptable approximation. This is not always true but is very often so.[103] When we are honest about the uncertainty of our parameters, it is easier to feel comfortable with the linear loss assumption.

The power of the staging methodology is that we can mix and match our aggregation. Parts can use linear loss and be fast. Parts can use Monte Carlo when necessary. These parts will run slower but will supply the required accuracy that the linear loss could not.

The entire model speeds up dramatically for two reasons. On the one hand, with the proper staging, very few parts of the model need to be Monte Carlo. A high proportion of the model can use the fast correlation matrix approach. On the other hand, the Monte Carlo portions themselves have fewer dimensions since they address fewer risk drivers. This means that a solution can be found much quicker.[104]

Tip 90: You may be able to get around a non-linear loss function by inserting a "dummy stage."

An example of this might be bond prices. We may feel comfortable that Principle Components Analysis (a linear model) is good for bond yields but we may not feel that bond prices are linear in those yields. Yields are linear but prices are not.

We can subdivide bond pricing into a lower (yields) stage and an upper (bond pricing) stage. Probably most implementations of principle components do something like this anyway. However, by explicitly subdividing the model we can capitalize on any run-time advantages.

The reason that this is an improvement is that the "dummy stage" can be nothing more than a yield to price function. The upper stage might be linear in the bond prices though it would not have been in the yields. If the distribution of yields from the lower model can be explicitly converted into a distribution of prices in the upper model, then it may be possible to perform a correlation matrix aggregation in the upper model using prices that we could not have done if we were using yields. Of course, this depends on the exact distribution of yields in the lower model.

Tip 91: Use more risk factors in your staged model.

Recall Tip 17: Do not worry about index proliferation (yet). The text leading up to that tip explained model enhancements that require more indices. For practitioners that use an entire Monte Carlo aggregation (what I call a Deathstar system) the increase of risk factors seemed infeasible, maybe even mad, as I described.

However, when we stage the entire aggregation, there is a huge leap in speed. With this in mind, we can design our entire model to have more risk factors as needed. Remember those advantages in Tip 12 through Tip 16? With a stage aggregation, we can incorporate these into our model. Without staging, this seemed infeasible. Staging allows an existing system to be much faster. More importantly, staging allows us to make even better models.

This appendix describes staging. It allows us to have the best of all modelling worlds.

By using a staged aggregation, the fact that this one module must be Monte Carlo means it is not that case that the whole model needs to be. Staging allows us to make one module be Monte Carlo if accuracy of that module is a concern. That module will be slower. However, just because this portion of the model is slower, we need not make other modules slower.

A staged method will be as slow as need be but no slower. A staged method is as accurate as uncertainty allows.

Appendix 4: Only as Good as your Loss Function

A major theme of this book has been that models should be reliable and quick. I have advocated that focusing on uncertainty mitigates the difficult trade-off between reliable and quick. By placing the uncertainty in our estimates in the limelight, we realize that "accurate" means "accurate within wide bounds of uncertainty." This insight allows us to speed up our models with easier assumptions.

This appendix explores a new dimension of uncertainty, one that is normally buried deep in a model and seldom brought to the light of day. In Appendix 1, Appendix 2 and Appendix 3, we saw that the loss function plays a major role in the trade-off between speed and accuracy. The loss function dictates which type of aggregation to use. The loss function gives rise to the Curve of Constant Loss. Our final aggregate capital estimate depends heavily on all the assumptions along the way. The start of that dependency chain is the loss function.

Tip 92: Realise how close the Correlation Matrix and a Monte Carlo approaches are in practice.

The basic aggregation methods of Appendix 2 show that all aggregations use the same basic eight steps.

Correlation matrix and Monte Carlo methods both use correlation matrices. Usually the same calibration can work for both methods. All the advantages and disadvantages of using correlation apply to both.[105] For example, each method uses a loss function, the focus of this appendix. Furthermore, both methods use heavy lifts to calibrate the standalone losses.

To contrast the two methods, the correlation matrix methods assume that the loss function is linear. Monte Carlo methods in current practice usually assume a polynomial function, which is more general. Both can be inaccurate. Many believe the polynomial loss function is massively superior to the linear assumption. This is not the case. Allow me to illustrate.

Even though Monte Carlo has a more general loss function, I would like to illustrate it is not general enough to make a sufficient impact. More research effort is needed in this area. Furthermore, staging helps our loss function modelling.

Consider a typical set-up. An insurer might have 25 risk factors. This is a low number in my experience. Many use 30, some circa 80 and I have even seen 150, but I use 25 in this example. How many coefficients are there in a 4th degree polynomial with 25 risk factors? In total, there are 23,751.[106] Even limiting ourselves to a 3rd degree polynomial (cubic) equation, this is 3,276 coefficients. Do we have this many points (heavy lifts) to fit all of these coefficients?

No. We have nowhere near enough information to calibrate a typical Monte Carlo aggregation. Running the actuarial models (the heavy lifts) is intensive work. Even the larger companies are hard pressed to get 100 runs in a month. This would be 300 runs each quarter, a tenth of what we need to fit accurately a cubic polynomial and less than 2% of that needed to fit a 4th degree polynomial.

Many good colleagues have attempted to fit formulas to loss points. The results are generally disappointing. It is not that there were not good people working on this. It is a difficult process, and the odds are against you to get a good fit. This is especially true when using a generic fitting function like a polynomial.[107] Though I have heard claims (rumours) that the fits used are "sufficient," no implementation that I am aware of has the actual practitioners being completely comfortable with the fits. Many are not satisfied at all.

This is only natural. If a company produces 300 heavy runs in a quarter, then using those to explore 20-30 dimensions of variability simply cannot work out. Even a modest number of cross terms will overwhelm the number of runs. There are just too many coefficients and too few runs to fit them.

If the fitted loss function is inaccurate, so are all the simulations that use it.

In fact, it is not as important that the Monte Carlo implementation has used a large number of scenario runs. Monte Carlo proponents are usually quick to say that 100,000 or 500,000 scenarios were tested. This is another case in which we should consider Tip 42: Don't lust after big N. There may have been hundreds of thousands of scenarios tested. However, they were tested against the fitted-formula, which relies on very few runs of actuarially sound systems. A chain is as weak as its weakest link and the weak link in Monte Carlo systems is the fitted loss function. The impact of an ill-fitted loss function could be significant, even if a large number of scenarios are used.

Tip 93: Do not Lust after Big N. (Monte Carlo version: Scenario testing is only as good as the fitted formula.)

If the fitted formula relies on only, say, 100 loss estimates that are trusted, then a Monte Carlo sampling of this should not have less uncertainty, at least not from the numbers alone. There may be reason to believe that these few runs are well placed. This might be combined with an argument that estimating between these runs (interpolation) is reliable. However, this is an expert judgement relying on more than simply the number of points. If you have reason to believe the formula fit is accurate, then that can give more confidence in the results from Monte Carlo sampling. Unfortunately, it is difficult to get that feeling of accuracy of a formula fit when the general form is simply a polynomial.

In the end, the practical implications of how many accurate runs (heavy lifts) are possible dictates the accuracy of a capital estimate. It is not so important how many scenarios we run against the formula-fitted loss function. What is crucially important is the answer to this question: how many accurate runs, how many heavy lifts, did we perform to calibrate the loss function?

Tip 94: With Monte Carlo, the number of Heavy lifts (in a detailed actuarial model) is more important than the number of scenarios tested against a formula-fitted function.

With Monte Carlo, do not focus on how many scenarios we run against a fitted formula. Focus on how many accurate heavy lifts we used in the creation of the formula fitted loss. This latter drives the uncertainty of the final capital requirement.

In both Monte Carlo and the correlation matrix approaches, there are Heavy lifts used to calibrate the model. After running the model, many practitioners perform at least one Heavy lift to confirm the answer for a killer scenario.[108] The important statistic is how many Heavy lifts we utilize in a meaningful way. In this manner, we can compare uncertainty between Monte Carlo calculations and correlation matrix calculations.

Consider the correlation matrix approach to show what I mean. A typical set-up might have 25 risk factors, a small "typical." As mentioned above, perhaps a good Monte Carlo implementation could manage to do 300 Heavy lifts in a quarter. How would a correlation matrix approach compare with this accuracy?

A basic correlation approach would only employ actuarial runs for the base case and standalone losses (one for each risk factor). Given 25 risk factors, this means 26 Heavy lifts. A basic correlation matrix approach uses the minimum number of runs. This minimum calibration (only 26 heavy lifts) indicates that this is the weakest possible aggregation methodology. Rather than utilizing the possible 300 runs, it only uses 26. This accounts for the low regard that many practitioners hold for this analysis.

The Standard Formula is a type of basic correlation matrix.

However, other than the Standard Formula, practitioners do not end the analysis after calculating the SCR from a correlation matrix. This figure is tested. The aggregated capital estimate from a correlation matrix is used to determine a killer scenario. This step might employ the Euler methodology. The killer scenario is run through a Heavy lift to see the true capital requirement in that scenario. Typically, there is a material difference.

Monte Carlo methods do the same thing, by the way. After testing 100,000 scenarios (or some other large number) using the fitted formula, the identified killer scenario is tested in an actuarial system, a heavy lift. This is usually done during calibration or testing the system, but may be skipped in a production environment. Typically, the heavy lift of a killer scenario is materially different from what the formula-fit loss function predicted.

Notice what this means. If the loss function was materially wrong, then the runs against the function (those 100,000 scenarios) were testing the wrong function. The killer scenario tested may be nowhere near a 1-in-200 event. This is a good time to let out a heavy sigh.

Tip 94 indicates that the loss function is the weakest link in the Monte Carlo analysis. No doubt, this has motivated the UK Institute and Faculty of Actuaries to establish a working party for formula fitting. (See Tip 65 in Chapter 10.)

I have advocated quick running models that allow more runs. Staging facilitates this. The ability to rerun models quickly allows us to determine sensitivity and build intuition about the model. If the model ran quickly, we could explore the difference in the capital estimate in the actuarial run of the killer scenario. However, Tip 94 emphasizes that the number of heavy runs is the actual constraining factor in our analysis. We are leading up to the next tip.

Tip 95: Know the assumptions your aggregation methods make about the shape of the Curve of Constant Loss.

Monte Carlo as currently used in practice assumes the Curve of Constant Loss to be a polynomial formula in the underlying factors. The correlation matrix assumes the relationship is a line.[109]

Both are wrong. One question is, "How wrong?" A better question is, "When is one method best and when is the other best?" This latter question is more open because it allows "best" to encompass more dimensions than just accuracy. For example, the correlation matrix approach is quicker to implement. We have seen that both have a high level of parameter uncertainty. I have advocated quickly run models for a host of reasons. Perhaps quick is the decisive factor in some situations. Of course a quick but entirely wrong model seems worse than useless. This is where staging allows us to compare accuracy to speed. Accuracy must be considered relative to parameter uncertainty. We cannot be more accurate than the certainty of our parameters.

Here again is this theme of quick versus accurate.

It is important to emphasize that the points used to calibrate the loss function are limited in practice. Each loss point represents a Heavy lift of an actuarial model. Tip 94 stressed that the number of potential Heavy lifts may be one of the main decisive factors in judging the quality of an aggregation. The next tip provides another crucial element.

Tip 96: Plan your Heavy lifts carefully to provide the maximum understanding of the Curve of Constant Loss.

Some applications use many detailed actuarial valuation runs (heavy lifts) for reasons other than calibrating the loss function. An attribution of capital to risk drivers via the Euler method is one reason. Given the central role of a loss function, especially in the Monte Carlo methodology, this seems misguided. As much of our actuarial capacity as possible should be focused on defining the loss function and its Curve of Constant Loss.

It is worth mentioning that there are different curves at different confidence levels. There is a Curve of Constant Loss at the 99.5% level, and a different one at the 90% level. Management may be interested in different quantile levels: a 1-in-200 loss, a 1-in-10 loss. While I speak of "a" or "the" Curve of Constant Loss, I mean with respect to a certain quantile level. In practice, the analysis must be repeated, at least in part, to determine the different quantile levels.

The placement, and not just the number, of heavy lifts forms a crucial component. We must be careful to choose accurate actuarial runs (Heavy lifts) that sufficiently estimate the Curve of Constant Loss.

I advocate a wide spread of Heavy lifts in order to understand the Curve of Constant Loss. If we cluster points too closely together, as done when using Euler for attribution, then the efficiency of our runs suffer. The closer one point is to other points, the less it contributes new information to the overall understanding of the Curve of Constant Loss.[110]

Correlation matrix implementations may also use Heavy lifts inefficiently. The reason is similar. After calibration and after performing the aggregation step, like in Monte Carlo, there is a Heavy lift to "true up" the answer. Without the perspective in this text, a practitioner performs this true up run with no intention to understand the Curve of Constant Loss.

Neither approach acknowledges that the need for a true up only underlines the shortcomings of the original loss function. If we truly were comfortable with the formula-fit loss function, a true up would not be necessary. This is why I advocate that all our heavy lift effort should be targeted at understanding the loss function and its implied Curve of Constant Loss. Attribution calculations and true-ups are luxuries given the uncertainty in the aggregate loss calculation.

The modelling of the loss function should be an exploration.

When using targeted Monte Carlo, target improving the formula-fit loss function, not getting closer to an initial loss function.

We can leverage our understanding analytically:

Tip 97: Not all calibrations to the Curve of Constant Loss require a heavy lift.

For example, the interest rate=0% scenario may be easy to calculate analytically.[111] Similarly, infinite interest rates leads to an easy analytic answer.[112] With some thought, many points can be determined. These count as heavy lifts.

Tip 98: Witnessing the results of some heavy lifts should inform the next heavy lift.

In a typical implementation, we could run a model, get a capital figure and get a killer scenario. I have indicated earlier that there is more than one killer scenario. There is an entire Curve of Constant Loss, not just a single killer scenario. Determine not just the one killer scenario, but instead several points along (or near) the Curve of Constant Loss.

Let us go further. For the estimated Curve of Constant Loss, we run some heavy lifts for points on this curve. Conceptually we could recalibrate the loss function. As it turns out, we only need to recalibrate the Curve of Constant Loss.[113]

Using the targeted Monte Carlo approach, we perform runs near this Curve of Constant loss. With this new run, we find the new Curve of Constant Loss. Call it Curve of Constant Loss-2. Then we use Curve of Constant Loss-2 to recalibrate our loss function and run again. With these results, we estimate a Curve of Constant Loss-3. We continue to get Curve of Constant Loss-4, a Curve of Constant Loss-5 and so forth. At some point, the loss function stabilizes and the Curve of Constant Loss also stabilizes. At that point, we can stop. The precise technical method for carrying out this updating is described in Endnote 89.

The final Curve of Constant Loss-N would be accurate. It would provide tremendous management information because there would be a number of killer scenarios identified.

To clarify this process further, allow me to compare it with the targeted Monte Carlo of Appendix 2. Tip 83 is similar to Tip 98. Tip 98 says we should perform heavy lifts in partitions. Targeted Monte Carlo divides up our simulations. Between each group of runs, we recalculated the Curve of Constant Loss, while keeping the loss function the same.

The above proposed methodology does the same calculations as targeted Monte Carlo but with an additional adjustment. After each group of runs, we update our loss function with the new heavy lifts before recalculating the Curve of Constant Loss.

This methodology is not without its potential limitations. One issue is how this methodology works when aggregating across business lines, products or legal entities. In this situation, there would be different loss functions and different curves of constant loss. This is discussed further in Tip 100.

We should redirect our focus to the loss function. Are the assumptions we make consistent with the heavy lifts we perform? Our precious heavy lift runs should concentrate on getting the form of the Curve of Constant Loss honed.

Tip 99: When staging, aggregate each risk factor only once.

If the staging is improperly designed, there can be difficulties. I illustrate the problem and a solution with an example.

Suppose we were modelling 3 different products. Each has a risk factor of equity and interest rates in common. Each product has 2 additional risk factors, but these are different for each product. To state it mathematically, let f_e be the equity risk factor, f_i be the interest rate risk factor, and the additional risk factors are $f_{1A}, f_{1B}, f_{2A}, f_{2B}, f_{3A}$ and f_{3B}, 8 risk factors in total. The loss function for each product $k \in \{1,2,3\}$ is given by the function: $Loss_k(f_e, f_i, f_{kA}, f_{kB})$. If we model the aggregation as one big correlation matrix, this would require $\binom{8}{2}=28$ correlation parameters.

We could however stage this analysis. Think of each aggregation as being a correlation matrix approach. We could have a second stage consisting of the 3 products and an overall stage that aggregates the 3 results of the products. Each of the 3 lower stages would be a 4 by 4 aggregation $\binom{4}{2}=6$ correlation parameters. There is some double counting here since the equity versus interest rate correlation appears in each of these 3 matrices. This means the total number of correlation parameters is $3x6 - 3 +1=16$. The upper stage, the aggregation, is a 3x3 which requires $\binom{3}{2}=3$ correlation parameters. Thus, the overall number of correlation parameters for this staging is $16+3=19$, which represents a savings in comparison with the 28 necessary for the large correlation matrix approach.

In theory, this is a savings. Is it really outside of theory? There are two issues here. First, we have essentially assumed correlations between the "additional" risk factors in different products, e.g. $cor(f_{1A}, f_{2A}), cor(f_{1A}, f_{2B}), cor(f_{1A}, f_{3A}), cor(f_{1A}, f_{3B}), cor(f_{1B}, f_{2A})$, and so on. This is 12 in total. We have had to consider these correlations in order to determine that they are zero. We have not reduced the number of correlations to consider. We have reduced the number to use in the calculation.

Notice that if these correlations were not zero, the entire staging design would be suspect. If these correlations were non-zero parameters, this separation into separate products may not be justified at all.

Assuming these across-product risk factors have zero correlation, the second issue deals with the fact that equity and interest rates appear in each of the product aggregations.

What does this mean for the 3 correlation parameters in the upper stage where the products are aggregated? How can we know these correlation parameters? Each of the 3 product losses is a function of equity and interest rates (among other risk factors). Depending on the nature of these loss functions, expressing the interaction as a correlation could be difficult. At the least, it would require separate analysis that may negate our savings in computation time. It would at least reduce our savings in computation.

The difficulty is that equity and interest rate aggregation takes place in each product in the lower stage. This is done 3 separate times in parallel. This parallel aggregation of the same risk factor is the problem. This is why Tip 99 says to aggregate each risk factor only once. Aggregating the same risk factor more than once in different portions of the model leads to problems, as illustrated in the above example.

The solution is to change the aggregation. At the lower stage, we aggregate over all variables except equity and interest rates. Rather than producing a loss figure in each product aggregation, we produce a new loss function. This new loss function is a function of only equity and interest rates. By taking the expectation over the "additional" risk, but not over equity and interest rates, we derive a new loss function *ELoss* that has as variables equity and interest rates.

Lower Stage (Product k) aggregation: $Loss_k(f_e, f_i, f_{kA}, f_{kB}) \mapsto ELoss_k(f_e, f_i)$

The aggregation at the upper stage is then simply aggregating the total of these expected losses over equity and interest rates.

Upper Stage Aggregation: aggregate $\sum_k ELoss_k(f_e, f_i)$ over f_e and f_i.

This methodology has 16 correlation parameters in the lower stage and 1 in the upper, a total of 17.

This methodology of this solution is more complicated. We must pass a formula of 2 variables from the lower stage to the higher stage.[114] Furthermore, we must express the uncertainty around this estimate. However, though theoretically complicated, practically, these direct changes should not cause significant difficulties. This is equally true for correlation matrix, Monte Carlo or mixed approaches.

The following and last tip of this appendix may be the most important.

Tip 100: Know the limitations of Staging.

New methodologies seem most promising before we place them in practice. For example, the use of linear models might seem to promise a solution in all cases. Large uncertainty justifies using a linear models (Tip 81) in most cases. The emphasis is in most case but not all cases. In Limitation 2 of Appendix 2, we gave an example of an operational risk model that led to a "right-angle" Curve of Constant Loss. A linear assumption would misrepresent this situation. Linear loss is not a panacea that we can use in every situation.

Though staging is not a new idea, it may be new to some readers. It is important to place it in context and to understand its limitations. The previous tip (Tip 99) indicated one limitation of staging. If there is material correlation between risk factors aggregated in same-stage modules, then there may be technical concerns. In some very complicated companies, it is conceivable that there may not be a satisfactory staging design. A poor implementation could erase the computational savings from Tip 85.

Another issue to challenge any aggregation, including a staged aggregation, is how to model between product lines, business units and separate entities. Different loss functions between products, business units and legal entities may give conflicting requirements for aggregation. The specifics of each company need to be considered in order to make an appropriate staging aggregation.

Fortunately, the savings in capital requirements provide the motivation for addressing these potential concerns. The spiral of capital savings (Tip 1) provides the means.

Appendix 5: Tips by Category

Motivation and the Spiral of Capital Savings
Tip 1, Tip 4, Tip 7, Tip 8, Tip 30

Organization of Team
Tip 9, Tip 29, Tip 50, Tip 53, Tip 54, Tip 56, Tip 57, Tip 59, Tip 74

Specific Ideas for generating Capital Requirements
Tip 11, Tip 12, Tip 13, Tip 14, Tip 15, Tip 16, Tip 18, Tip 20, Tip 20, Tip 22, Tip 23, Tip 24, Tip 25, Tip 26, Tip 75, Tip 76

Model Design (not Aggregation)
Tip 10, Tip 17, Tip 27, Tip 28, Tip 45, Tip 46, Tip 47, Tip 48, Tip 49, Tip 51, Tip 52, Tip 68, Tip 71, Tip 72, Tip 73, Tip 79

Aggregation Specific Tips concerning Model Design
Tip 80, Tip 81, Tip 82, Tip 83, Tip 84, Tip 85, Tip 86, Tip 87, Tip 88, Tip 89, Tip 90, Tip 91, Tip 92, Tip 93, Tip 94, Tip 95, Tip 96, Tip 97, Tip 98, Tip 99, Tip 100

Doubting Established Models
Tip 31, Tip 32, Tip 33, Tip 34, Tip 35, Tip 36, Tip 37, Tip 38, Tip 93

Knowing Uncertainty
Tip 39, Tip 40, Tip 41, Tip 42, Tip 43, Tip 44, Tip 48, Tip 78, Tip 81, Tip 82

Typical Objections Addressed
Tip 58, Tip 59, Tip 60, Tip 61, Tip 62, Tip 63, Tip 64

Big Picture
Tip 21, Tip 55, Tip 65, Tip 66, Tip 67, Tip 69, Tip 70, Tip 76, Tip 77

Tips that work for Standard Formula:
Tip 4, Tip 11, Tip 12, Tip 13, Tip 14, Tip 15, Tip 16, Tip 18, Tip 20, Tip 21, Tip 22, Tip 23, Tip 24, Tip 25, Tip 26, Tip 30, Tip 38, Tip 71, Tip 75, Tip 76, Tip 79, Tip 82.

Endnotes:

[1] With a unit-linked product, the leverage is high. If you ignore the fixed costs of being in business and the funded expenses (such as commissions for selling), the leverage is infinite since the equity is zero. If you count the costs of being in business, then there is a positive equity amount. The leverage is still high, but it is not infinite.

[2] I am not the first to say this. For example, Christopher Hursey and Rebecca Scott said, "This is not just about compliance," in Section 2.1 of "Replicating Formulae: Efficient Calibration Techniques," Presented at the Staple Inn (UK) Actuarial Society 7th February 2012.

[3] This may not be entirely new, given the parallels to gross premium reserves. However, the scale of the implications in Solvency II is significant.

[4] As a caveat, this book is not a reference manual of all things relating to Solvency II. Other more standard aspects of Solvency II have been covered in other contexts and may well change. The focus here is the main issues to consider if your goal is to generate capital.

[5] With this analogy though, I risk inappropriate imagery since the "random searching for connections" aspects associated with puzzles has no counterpart in creating an Internal Model. In fact, the process starts with knowing the connection you wish to make then building the pieces that match.

[6] I would like to say again that this is a contentious area. Some actuaries and risk managers state the sentiment that we should focus on identifying the amount of capital that we "need to hold," not specifically the amount we are "required to hold." The "need to hold" is an economic necessity. The "required to hold" is a regulatory requirement. It is as if anyone who speaks of capital "requirement" is automatically trying to game the system. This is an understandable view in the previous regimes, in which "necessary capital" and "regulatory capital" may not be the same. It is generally accepted that there could have been a difference between meeting regulation and having enough capital for "real reasons." However, this is the primary way in which Solvency II has changed the entire industry, the entire game if you will.

In Solvency II, the "required" capital from regulations arises from an assessment of the "necessary" capital from an economic view. With proper risk management, there is no distinction between required and necessary. If anyone tells you otherwise, then something is out of line, either with their view or the actual capital model.

In practice, there may be a difference in judgement between management, regulators and professional experts. The regulatory requirement provides a firm measure. This is especially true if your company only uses the standard formula. Even with an Internal Model, the model must be approved by the regulator and so it provides a firm target.

The conclusion is that: Required capital is acceptable as a basis for measuring incentives.

[7] If you are able to get 50bp on the difference between the A and AAA ratings, and your capital was 5% of total assets, then your liabilities are 24 times as large as your own capital. So, your return on owner's equity (capital) is:

RoE: = (rate earned on assets backing capital) + 24 x 0.5%
= (rate earned on assets backing capital) + 12%

With this, it is quite easy to earn more than the 15% target many US companies target.

[8] Using the example from the previous note, suppose the assets backing your liabilities had a modified duration that is 1 larger than your liabilities when interest rates rose 1%. Now, your assets lose 1% more than your liabilities. Assuming the assets backing capital did not lose any value, this rise in interest rates means you lost 0.96% of total assets. However, 0.96% of assets is 19.2% of capital (= 0.0096 / .05), a loss

of almost 20%. That is a real risk. The point is that a spread strategy requires a very tight match. There is also no room for assets that have call options (against the bondholder), or any other type of variation really.

[9] When Solvency II began, I was amazed at how many consultants claimed Solvency II experience, in the sense that "we have done this before." It is okay to say you have applicable experience. But to claim direct experience seems a bald face lie. After all, no one had. The regulations were not complete and still are being developed at this time. Claims of actually having done it (as opposed to applicable experience) seemed overstated, to say the least. Few people called them on it. It put some of us (me) at a competitive disadvantage since my wording always tried to be more accurate: I have done market consistent balance sheets for 23 years; I have done asset-liability management for a similar time; I have taught stochastic calculus and written Monte Carlo and asset-liability management systems, QIS 5 experience etc. All the elements necessary for Solvency II, but without claiming to have done it.

What is the next thing these credible consultants said? "It will probably cost £100 million to implement Solvency II." Rather than detail discussions of what would be gotten for that amount, a company more often than not simply started ramping up, expanding budgets (releasing a little of the conservative assumptions perhaps so that the capital would be there), and hiring "managers" who in many cases knew little or nothing about solvency to fill up the huge budget amounts.

[10] Richard Branson, "Business Stripped Bare," Virgin Books, P23.

[11] International Financial Reporting Standards.

[12] Own Risk and Solvency Assessment.

[13] If "job security" is the answer for why others should lower capital, you are using only the stick and not carrot. It is not the best way to motivate people. While a stick could get some motion out of a donkey to move, a carrot truly motivates innovation.

[14] Actually, the Star Wars saga had two Deathstars that blew up, one in Episode 4 and one in Episode 6.

[15] Mixing my science fiction metaphors, perhaps all Deathstar systems should have "the words DON'T PANIC inscribed in large friendly letters on the cover." It would not make them safer, just less scary.

[16] Richard Engel actually was his name.

[17] We employed what would later be called a "whole balance sheet" approach. This meant that we modelled all the assets in the company. This is a Solvency II standard. If truth be told, I never "got" the idea for excluding assets backing capital. I guess capital management was always in my blood. I view myself as a custodian of both policyholders' and shareholders' money. In a mutual, this may be more obvious than in a shareholder company. These stakeholders have different expectations and requirements. Excluding assets backing shareholder capital form my analysis always feels inappropriate since I must care for those assets as well.

[18] I am discussing stand-alone events, here, assuming only one-risk variable (e.g. equity price levels) changes.

[19] Ways to exclude 1974 in an analysis of the UK equity market:

   1. Political analysis:
       a. the turmoil in the UK in 1974 was unprecedented: a 3-day workweek to cope with lack of energy,
       b. the increase of the marginal tax rate to 83%,
       c. the end of the Bretton Woods system 3 years earlier,
       d. High inflation (~20%).

This general argument states that even though it happened historically, it could never (in a 1-in-200 kind of way) happen again.
2. Use of Q-Q or P-P plots to show it an outliner.
3. Use of statistics tests which tend to smooth out the tail.
4. Use natural diversification of the portfolio, as discussed in the text.

[20] Chapter 5 discusses the uncertainty of such estimates. The stress you use might be a little higher to account for the uncertainty. However, this applies equally to both the 49% and the 36% estimates mentioned in the text.

[21] The stress mentioned in the text is the standalone equity capital. In practice, the aggregated capital affect would be less than the standalone effect. For example, an £18m reduction in equity standalone capital might mean only a £12m reduction in aggregate capital. Accordingly, the calculation of cost of capital might be different, i.e. 8.3% = 1 / 12. This is still an attractive rate.

I have left off the aggregation portion of the calculation to allow this early section of the book to flow. The conclusion with the aggregated capital calculation (as it should be done) still remains that the strategy in Tip 15 is an attractive possibility.

[22] The annualized costs of options go down for longer maturities. For example, if an at-the-money 1-year option costs 10, and an at-the-money 5-year option costs 25, the annualized cost for the first is 10 (= 10/1) and for the second is 5 (=25/5). The longer dated option covers the risk for longer and on an amortized basis is cheaper.

This could be made even cheaper by a program that buys long options and sells them after a year to be replaced by a new long option. The strategy focuses on the small price decay in the early years of an option (much less that 5 for the above 5 year option). However, coordinating this with the liquidity of options and bid-ask spreads and changing market levels requires specialist knowledge. These are not particularly involved tasks, nor are they breaking new ground, but this is a specialist area and not detailed here.

[23] In this case, the benefit is not as dramatic as with the equity diversification. In the equity diversification, a non-diversified index (the UK) was compared with a diversified international portfolio. In this instance, moving from the UK-only to the diversified international index had a dramatic reduction in the final stress. In Tip 16, however, corporate stresses are usually defined relative to a spread index, say, the single A-corporate bond spread. This is already a diversified index, typically diversified over different sectors by some weighting like market capitalization. The large benefit for moving from a non-diversified index to a diversified index will not be realized by looking at the detail of corporate spreads by sector.

However, there is a realized benefit by changing the weights used to make the index. One can always do better than a static weighting driven by a static rule such as weighting by market capitalization. Admittedly, this is smaller than a true diversification benefit but give the size of most companies credit risk, this can be worthwhile to consider.

[24] Using concepts from later in the book, this equity analysis forms a separate module. Its aggregation is a linear model. It is perfectly represented by a correlation matrix approach.

[25] Rather than reducing required capital, we could try to get the best return on existing capital. By this, I mean (required capital) plus (Own Funds). In general, we would like to earn a required return on Own Funds as well as required capital. The entire book assumes that we wish to lower capital requirements in general. This is a strategic goal. On a day-to-day basis, it may be more reasonable to consider the total capital (required + Own Funds) as a fixed number and make as much as we can with that.

[26] A hedge equity position can have similar characteristics to a corporate bond.

The hedge goes like this:

If you bought all 100 shares in the FTSE 100 with the right weights and shorted a FTSE 100 future, then you would have no equity exposure. What you would get is a synthetic fixed rate instrument. Conceptually, the net effect of this is "zero", but in practice such a combination would provide a fixed rate of return.

This fixed return is a short rate. It is comparable to a swap rate for a maturity that is the same maturity as the future used. (This assumes you roll over the futures at each maturity.) The effect is that a program of selling futures versus an equity portfolio produces a floating rate fixed rate. The rate floats with a frequency appropriate to the maturity of the future contract used.

This synthesized floating rate security can be swapped to a long, floating rate via a fixed-for-floating swap. Up to this point, we have created a synthetic, long, fixed instrument that is essentially a bond.

The new risk dimension (providing extra return) goes like this:

Now consider shorting futures against an equity portfolio and using the fixed-for-floating swap to get the proper maturity as above. However, the equity portfolio is not exactly the same index as represented in the future's index. We introduce basis risk by using a portfolio slightly different from the index. Deviating from the index allows a fund manager to take a position in order to out-perform the index. A good manager should be able to out-perform the index in order to provide an expected extra return.

This extra return due to out-performing the index plays the role of a corporate spread. It adds expected return by introducing a dimension of risk.

Since the risk taken is different from the credit risk, if we reduce our exposure to corporate bonds and replace it with this synthetic strategy, then we should have a diversification benefit on our final capital.

Three comments on this strategy usually come to mind:

1. There could be periods in which the selection strategy under-performs the index – a bad quarter, say. This mirrors the same risk in bonds, in which a period in which credit spreads widening would have corporate bonds under-perform risk-free (or swap based) bonds.
2. Not all managers can be expected to out-perform the equity market. This again mirrors the risk in corporate bonds in which some portfolios have default losses that remove any gains from spreads. In both equity selection and credit selection, you must have good managers.
3. The amount of allowable variation from the index can be set by management so that the risk incurred from any stock selection (away from the index) is comparable to the risk incurred for investing in any corporate bond.

[27] To generate capital, we must try to increase the amount of Own Funds, the amount of assets above both liability reserves and required capital. This causes a technical wrinkle when discussing VIF. The Solvency Capital Requirement (SCR), according to the Solvency II standard formula, should capture the 1-in-200-year interest rate risk of a firm's assets and best estimate liabilities only. Notice that Risk Margin is not considered in determining SCR. However, if the value of the Risk Margin changes, this will change the reserve liability, and in so doing, the Own Funds of the company are affected. We must be a little careful when describing what we wish to manage.

In the end, we wish to manage to have high Own Funds. In almost all cases, this means we wish to reduce SCR. The Risk Margin should also be managed. To generate capital, we wish to lower (and keep low) the SCR while making sure that Risk Margin does not have a high variability.

[28] See Brave Partners, "Solvency II: A Whiff of VIF, August 2010.

[29] Music royalties (using songs in films, or playing the on the radio, not specific albums or recording) generally are renegotiated by the international industry every 3 years. It is not as regular as the annual reset of inflations swaps, and not as specific to a particular inflation index, but still quite credible for long requirements like fixed benefit pensions.

[30] Solvency II requires that the capital model be used by the company. The company must prove that it was not simply "another report in the room." Many companies find this proof a challenge. When the capital model is made as simply a financial reporting exercise, the Use Test can be daunting indeed.

[31] 99tipsfeedback@financial-guard.co.uk or matt.modisett@financial-guard.co.uk.

[32] Jason Zweig, "How the Big Brains Invest at TIAA-CREF", Money, 27(1), p114, January 1998.

[33] Suppose a person is facing a large loss, say £1 million, with certainty that would bankrupt him. Suppose he has two investments: A yields £100,000 with certainty, while B yields £2 million with a 2% chance and zero with a 98% chance. The expected value of A is greater than that of B, and its variance is zero which is lower than B. A rational person could choose B, even though its expected return is lower and variance (risk) is higher. At least with B, he has a chance of avoiding default. Is that irrational? This is the opposite from what theory would say.

Another example comes from market consistent models. Consider a stock for which we assume the return is lognormal. This is actually a consequence of the Black-Scholes model, but this assumption of returns arises in many contexts. Let us say that the associated normal variable has mean μ and standard deviation σ. The expected value of the lognormal variable, X, is $E(X) = e^{\mu + \sigma^2/2}$. With this, we can see that the expected value of the lognormal variable is higher for greater variability. If two securities had the same lognormal mean, a "rational" investor could prefer that riskier investment since it has a higher expected value.

[34] It almost seems a precursor to today. I wonder if financial historians will eventually look at the Long Term Capital Management deal as some sort of watershed moment, when central banks had to expand their concepts of themselves in order to continue with their mandated raison d'etre: to defend the values of bank balance sheets.

[35] From Wikipedia, http://en.wikipedia.org/wiki/Long-Term_Capital_Management.

[36] Select a series of (vanilla) options that are identical in every way except for strike: same maturity, same underlying, and same type (put or call). If you graph the implied volatility of each, the theory says you should get a horizontal line. After all, the volatility is a function of the underlying security, not the option. It might vary for different time periods, but since we have chosen options that have the same time to maturity, the volatility should be the same. That is the assumptions of the model. However, we do not get a horizontal line. Here are some samples of what we get:

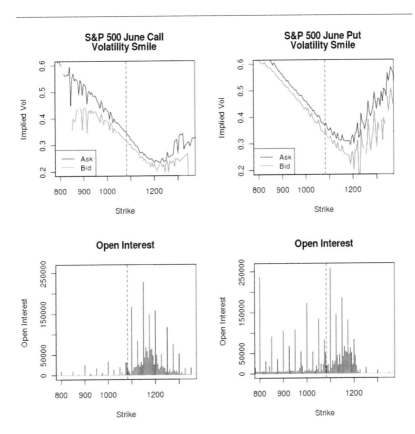

Above, the top 2 graphs are the implied volatilities for June contracts, put and call, while the lower graphs are the associated open-interest graphs. As you can see, the open interest volume is greater for strikes that are multiples of 50. Whether or not you focus on the strikes with greater open interest, it is clear that the implied volatility for different strikes is not a constant. This U shape is the volatility smile. There are also smirks, which are flat on one side, but still not constant. It is worth emphasizing that the index is a liquid one and that this aberration cannot be the result of sparse trading interest in some obscure share. In fact, the prevalence of the smile is ubiquitous, appearing in options for different countries, different types of security (shares, currencies, bonds) and has persisted over decades.

Why is this a problem? The volatility is supposedly a characteristic of the underlying share (or currency or whatever) and not specific to the option in question. That the volatility changes from option to option when there is no other difference in the underlying shows there to be a flaw in the overall theory. The prices of the options, as displayed in the implied volatilities, in practice do not conform to the theory.

Therefore, the theory is wrong. Period. There have been a number of models that try to correct this. Jump diffusion and the like. None of them have gotten universal acceptance.

[37] I use the "forward" contract for simplicity rather than a futures contract. The futures contract has margin calls, which could complicate the discussion. The forward contract has a single payment at expiration equal to (forward price less price at expiration). The conclusions are the same for futures as well as forwards.

[38] Said in a calculus way, the success of asset-liability management depends on correctly calculating the first derivative or higher order derivatives. Setting the capital requires us to get the non-differentiated function correct.

Remember in calculus exams always getting -1 point because you forgot to add "+C" to the end of an integration. For example:

Problem: $dy = f(x)dx$

Solution: $y = F(x) + C$

The "C" is the constant of integration and could be anything. You generally needed some sort of initial conditions to be able to find C.

The Solvency II equivalent is that asset-liability management methods need something more to be able to calculate capital amounts; some form of "initial conditions" are needed to set the "C".

[39] For further discussion, see also Aswath Damodaran, "Into the Abyss: What if nothing is risk free?" http://pages.stern.nyu.edu/~adamodar/pdfiles/papers/nothingisriskfree.pdf.

[40] It is interesting to read the original paper on Black-Scholes and to examine their choice of short rate. They do not use the term risk-free rate, rather simply state that the "short rate is known". The mathematical derivation uses the concept of hedging the position continuously, a process that requires borrowing and investing in the underlying stock (for a participant replicating a long call position, for example). Thus, the short-term rate is clearly talking about a borrowing rate.

Can we borrow at the risk-free rate? Maybe from our parents (biological or financial) but in general, the answer is, "no." So, the foundations of the Black-Scholes model itself indicate that a rate higher than a governmental rate is the appropriate basis for the short rate assumption.

As an aside, we could use the Black-Scholes pricing convention to determine r, the rate in the model, and σ, the volatility. We could allow r to vary with strike and σ to be a single parameter across all strikes. This would lead to and "r-smile" with a flat volatility assumption. This would satisfy the Black-Scholes theory. The σ is fixed for a series of options with the r being the parameter that takes up the difference across strikes. In this manner, the contradiction between theory and practice can be avoided. The r is not a general r as we see it today, a background parameter for all securities (the "risk-free rate") rather a borrowing rate specific to the company doing a delta hedge. We could even imagine a routine to fit mathematically the closest r-smile and volatility.

Furthermore, the fact that different strikes have a different associated short rate could be explained by either:

1.   Segmentation: different players participate in different strikes (moneyinesss). They have different cost of capital giving rise to different short rates used in the pricing of the options they offer for sale.

2.   Higher spreads required for lower volume trades: in this version, a single participant may write options at different strikes. To cover their cost of capital (for margins against delta-hedge

strategies and for writing the option), the participant builds in a price margin to any option they write. This price margin is directly related to their cost of capital (which could be a high number like 15% or 30%, as many derivative houses require). The perceived time for holding the option affects the price mark-up. I say perceived time since the option may not be held to maturity, especially those options whose strikes have higher volumes. These players view the higher volume options to have a shorter holding time because they perceive that other players will take the position off their hands sooner. Accordingly, the price premium for these options is less; conceptually it is amortized over a shorter period. Using the Black-Scholes pricing formula as a pricing convention, the extra (reduced) price premium translates directly into an increased (reduced) implied volatility. It would also seem that the low premium of out of the money options would incur a proportionally higher margin costs, and as such, the extra premium demanded by option writers would have a proportionally larger effect on more out-of-the money or in-the-money options.

The above has the possibility of salvaging the Black-Scholes theory without heroic models of jump volatility or similar models. It is also a supply-demand driven model, which is attractive form the standpoint of bringing modern finance back into alliance with economics. There is a price associated with this line of reasoning, however; the concept of risk-free return needs to be abandoned or at least modified. Fortunately, the market appears to be reviewing the concept of risk-free because of the current financial crisis.

[41] In mathematics, if s is the nominal spread (e.g. 0.75%), which is composed of d (expected defaults, e.g. 0.25%) and e (excess spread above defaults, e.g. 0.50%), then we have s = e + d. We require that :

$$(1+s)(1-d) > 1,$$

which is a rewording of the positive expectation assumption.

Let n equal the number of bonds. Using a normal distribution approximation, choose a confidence interval for which you would like to have a positive return over governmental bonds, say 99%. (The "Z" for this is 2.33.) Expected excess return for n bonds = $n((s+1)(1-d)-1)=n(s-sd-d)=n(s(1-d)-d)=n(e-sd)$ [This assumes no recovery from defaults.] Variance of excess return for n bonds = $n(1-d)ds^2 = \sigma^2$ [This assumes no recovery from defaults.]

Prob(excess return > 0) = .99% => $n(s(1-d)-d) - Z \sigma n^{0.5} > 0$
⇨ $(s(1-d)-d) - Z \sigma n^{-0.5} > 0$

As long as s(1-d) –d> 0 (as assumed), one can find n large enough to insure the above inequality.

[42] More food for thought: if there is no risk-free rate, what exactly does this mean for a matching adjustment calculation? (Matching adjustment used to be called Illiquidity Premium but the industry thinking has moved evolved.)

[43] Market Consistent values are calculated in each simulation. To determine which simulations to use, real world scenarios are used. The figure is from Laurent Devineau, and Stéphane Loisel, "Risk aggregation in Solvency II: How to converge the approaches of the Internal Models and those of the Standard Formula,"

[44] I have changed the actual numbers. The closeness of the numbers is well represented.

[45] Again, I changed the actual numbers while keeping the range representative.

[46] See for example from TAS M, A.1.1, C.4.11, C.5.2, from TAS R A.1.1, C.4.3, C.5.2-4, and from TAS D A.1.1, and C.3.2.

[47] Ralph Frankland; Andrew D Smith; Timothy Wilkins; Elliot Varnell; Andy Holtham; Enrico Biffis; Seth Eshun; David Dullaway "Modelling extreme Market Events: a Report of the Benchmarking Stochastic Models Working Party," Presented to the Institute of Actuaries, 3 November 2008, and the Faculty of Actuaries, 19 January 2009, Institute and Faculty of Actuaries.

[48] I use December-to-December returns for my equity analysis. I do this to avoid the complicating wrinkle of considering different month ends, to keep the presentation complexities at a minimum. If you are interested in the different month-end issue, see Tip 78.

[49] I assumed a lognormal variable. I assumed for simplicity that the mean is zero and the standard deviation is the size to make the 0.5% quantile a (simple) return of -49%. I modeled using log-returns but all my figures presented here are simple returns.

[50] Furthermore, in this analysis, I have used fixed parameters for the distributions. The extreme Events Working Party rightly included the uncertainty of the parameters in their thinking. This effect increases uncertainty further.

[51] Bernard Bosanquet, "The Meeting of extremes in Contemporary Philosophy, London, 1921, p. 100 as quoted in Fredrick von Hayek's "Counter Revolution of Science: Studies on the Abuse of Reason," Free Press of Glencoe, Collier-Macmillan, London, 1955, p195.

[52] Purists may complain here. By using the extremes of 16 and 48 to calculate the extremes of the diversified capital, they would say that I have not properly accounted for the diversification effect. There might be a high end on one side and a low end on the other side, offsetting to some extent.

For example, if our two standalone risk variables are I and C, each of which is N(32,8) and the correlation is 50%, then the variable T=I + C is N(64, σ) where $\sigma = \sqrt{8^2 + 8^2 + 2 \times .5 \times 8 \times 8} = 13.8$. If the relative certainty were proportional, as in the text, then σ should be 16. Since it is smaller, some reduction of risk has taken place in the diversification.

There is validity in this argument, if we are comfortable with the analogy to Normal distributions. The above discussion is not saying that the loss is Normal. Instead, it is saying that our uncertainty of the actual stress level is a Normal variable. This is different. Furthermore, I have used 50% correlation above. This is a common misconception. The correlation between losses in the text is 50%. The correlation between our uncertainties in the stresses I and C could be something different. There is no reason defacto to have any idea at all what correlation to use. On a more general level, there is little objective reason to use the Normal distribution, or any other distribution, for the stresses.

This entire line of reasoning can be recast in the debate between Bayesian Statistics and Frequentist Statistics. Actuaries are trained in the latter. If they learn the former, it is from outside the actuarial training process. It might be done as continuing professional development, but even then, the actuary would have to choose this area. The frequentist approach assumes that the parameter (like our stress above) is fixed. The Bayesian does not view it as fixed, rather as an unknown that has its own distribution. The assignment of the distributions is a source of criticism of the Bayesian approach: the distribution (in particular the prior distribution) is arbitrary, and cannot be objectively decided. Ironically, the frequentist assumption of a fixed parameter says the parameter has a point distribution, and this assumption can be criticized on the exact same arbitrary grounds.

Needless to say, this debate is outside of the scope of this text. The position in the text is valid when one realises the assumptions that must be necessarily made to try to prove/demonstrate that uncertainty is reduced.

[53] Good examples of how correlations can vary significantly, according to what time periods are selected, as provided in R.A. Shaw, A.D. Smith and G.S. Spivak's paper, "Measurement and Modelling of Dependencies in Economic Capital," a discussion paper presented to the Institute of Actuaries, 10 May 2010.

[54] The estimate used for correlations standard deviation is the Fisher transform. If r is the calculated correlation for X ad Y, then the transform is defined as $z = \frac{1}{2} \ln\left(\frac{1+r}{1-r}\right)$. If X and Y have a bivariate Normal distribution then z is approximately Normally distributed. The standard error for z is $\frac{1}{\sqrt{N-3}}$.

Armed with the inverse formula $r = \frac{\exp(2z)-1}{\exp(2z)+1}$ can be used to find the confidence interval of r.

The text says that r has the standard error $\frac{1}{\sqrt{N-3}}$, but this is only an approximation.

[55] Star Wars, Episode 4: a New Hope came out over 30 years ago, but compared with the Bible's publication date, I can call Star Wars modern.

[56] It seems so long ago now to contemplate how a mere 7 scenarios was a regulatory challenge for insurers.

[57] By the way, some of the specialists deal with the connections between specialists. For example the general ledger booking systems deals with connections to the portfolio managers system. In this sense, I use "specialist" in the text in the most general sense of the word: anyone touching an aspect of analysis.

[58] Some readers might consider cases of wilful fraud to be inappropriate examples to illustrate breakdown in risk processes. I sympathise with the view. Still, lapse in morality is one of the risks that should be caught in a process, even if perpetrated by high-level individuals.

[59] Commutation functions were the manner in which actuaries performed complex calculations before computers. It would be interesting if they offer insight into a computer problem as well.

The theory of commutation functions say that different factors can be expressed in vectors. Using the well-known sum-product function from Excel provides the prototypical calculation. We choose vectors of factors over time for different intervals. For example, we would have a discount vector, survival, continuation and so on. A typical set might be (the indices denote time through a scenario):

Discount vector: $(D_1, D_2, ..., D_n)$

Survival vector: $(l_1, l_2, ..., l_n)$

Persistency: $(p_1, p_2, ..., p_n)$

Schedule of Face $(F_1, F_2, ..., F_n)$ (These may all be equal if the face amount is constant.)

Other factors could be included.

The present value of these variables is the sum-product of these vectors (t is the time variable):

$$PV = \sum_{t=1}^{N} D_t l_t p_t F_t$$

179

The interesting thing is that each vector could be simplified in practice by using piecewise approximations. For example, suppose the model for interest rates had a flat yield curve, i.e. one interest rate and $D_t = (1 + r)^{-t}$. We might be able to model the discount vector as a piecewise linear vector in the following manner. Choose s particular model interest rate points. $r_1 < r_2 < \ldots < r_s$. These lead to s different discount vectors:

$$\left((1 + r_1)^{-1}, \ldots, (1 + r_1)^{-N} \right)$$
$$\left((1 + r_2)^{-1}, \ldots, (1 + r_2)^{-N} \right)$$
$$\vdots$$
$$\left((1 + r_s)^{-1}, \ldots, (1 + r_s)^{-N} \right)$$

Note, these are scalar vectors since we have chosen $r_1 < r_2 < \ldots < r_s$ to be scalars. If $r_1, r_2, \ldots, r_s$ are chosen well, then the linear approximation between $\left((1 + r_j)^{-1}, \ldots, (1 + r_j)^{-N} \right)$ and $\left((1 + r_{j+1})^{-1}, \ldots, (1 + r_{j+1})^{-N} \right)$ well approximates $\left((1 + r)^{-1}, \ldots, (1 + r)^{-N} \right)$ when $r_j < r < r_{j+1}$. By using a linear approximation of each vector, the analysis would be easier. Likely the commutation function would be well-behaved.

Of course, this would be more complicated since each vector might have several parameters. Interest rates might be modelled with a PCA analysis. These typically have 3 components. Accordingly, there would be 3 PCA factors, each with an associated piecewise estimate. Perhaps rather than a normal PCA analysis in which each yield is a linear function of PCA components, perhaps we could arranged that each component corresponds to a different discount factor.

Likewise, each other vector (lapse, survival) might be a function of different factors.

[60] This is discussed in Donald F. Behan and Samuel H. Cox's paper, "A Procedure for Simulation with Constructed Copulas" American Academy of Actuaries Report to NAIC, Correlation period 1978-1996, December 1997.

[61] The margin requirements of the exchange primarily account for its increased standing as counterparty.

[62] Even if the exchange is the insurance company's counterparty, typically the other leg of the transaction goes to an investment bank as counterparty. The exchange merely stands between the insurer and bank. The exchange does not take the risk of the transaction. It simply stands between the counterparties, protecting each from the other's credit risk. The exchange's credit risk is covered via margin or collateral accounts.

[63] Another technical issue is lapsation and how it relates to the form of the product. For example, if the product were structured as a straight swap on gas prices, the company paying floating to the customer and receiving fixed, the company would be exposed to a one sided risk: if prices move against the company so that the policyholder was a net payer, the policyholder would lapse the product. This would leave the company with a loss, and potentially a large one.

The solution is to provide an attractive guarantee to keep the policyholder from leaving. Something like, "Your price will never go up but can go down." This is a guarantee-laden contract that would need to be offset with an option on gas or with a delta-neutral hedge to replicate the option. These require specialist skills but nothing particularly unusual. We can find people to do this hedge.

This would likely complicate the product sale, though we can manage this too. The issue is that we must fund the option premium. This is true whether we hedge with an actual option or if we delta-hedge. The initial price that the customer pays would need to be higher than the current price. For illustration, suppose this mark up is 10%. (I have done no analysis to estimate this.) Now the sales presentation is something like this:

> "Initially you pay 10% more for gas than you do now. 'Why should you pay more for something?' you ask. Well, this price will never go up. This illustration shows how much it has varied in the past. Furthermore, if prices move down, so will your price. You will be locking in lower prices as they arise. Eventually, you will have a nice locked in low price. This illustration shows that with price movements from recent years, if you had taken this policy [T] years ago, you would be below the current price by [y] % (even after the 10% adjustment)."

This means the initial clients might need to be more sophisticated. After the product had a track record, less sophisticated clients would also feel comfortable.

As you can see, technical issues arise, and their solutions might have knock-on effects to other issues. All of these are manageable.

[64] I personally like these types of products. The "common man" should not be subject to the gyrations of the market when it comes to staple goods (such as food and energy). However, past political solutions that attempt to fix prices have ended badly.

This new product offers fixed prices for staple to the common man but does so using market mechanisms. The price management is performed by a sophisticated institution that can handle it. The common man would otherwise be in no positions to manage this risk. He has neither the necessary skills nor the economies of scale to do energy and food price hedging.

Meanwhile, the producers are still subjected to price variation. All of the positive aspects of price gyrations, namely competition fostering innovation, remain in-tack. This seems the best of all worlds: capitalist competition to drive innovation combined with protection from market gyrations for the common man for staple goods.

[65] The text refers to such test as goodness of fit test (e.g. Kolmogorov-Smirnov, Anderson Daring, and Shapiro-Wilk test), tests for skewness (D'Aostino's test), kurtosis (Anscombe's test) and others statistics such as higher moments' estimate or errors.

[66] Recall that if two variables are independent, then their correlation must be zero. (Not all zero-correlated variables are independent.) If you have two variables with a high positive correlation (or very negative one) then for sure they are not independent.

[67] From http://www.marioguerrero.info/154/readings/Squire.pdf, Peverill Squire, "Why the 1936 Literary Digest Poll Failed."

[68] The paper concludes,

> "The evidence presented here strongly supports the conclusion that the 1936 Literary Digest poll failed to project the correct vote percentages or even the right winner not simply because of its initial sample, but also because of a low response rate combined with a nonresponse bias."

The initial sample and nonresponse bias are evidence of sample dependence.

[69] There is a thorny technical clarification to make here. Annual non-overlapping returns could be dependent. For example, a year of down returns could lead to up returns. Alternatively, trends from year to year might exist. Non-overlapping data may still have annual returns with some dependence.

If we perform auto correlation analysis on overlapping data, we get 1-month lags of over 90%. This clearly violates the independence requirement for statistical tests.

However, if we perform similar autocorrelation analysis on non-overlapping data, the best estimate correlation is not exactly zero. When we consider the possible error in the correlation analysis (e.g. using Fischer's transform) we cannot, to this author's experience, reject the hypothesis that the correlation is zero. This is the basis of the claims in the text. It would be inaccurate, however, to say that the annual non-overlapping series are known to be independent, in any provable way. The weight of the evidence is in favour of the non-overlapping series, but in statistics, we can never be absolutely sure.

We can say in any instance that the violations of the assumptions for statistical tests is either no violation for non-overlapping data, or to a degree considerably lower than for overlapping data.

[70] For further discussion see: Ardian Harri, B. Wade Vrorsen, "The overlapping Data Problem," Quantitative and Qualitative Analysis in Social Sciences, Volume 3, Issue 3, 2009, 78-115, ISSN: 1752-8925. http://qass.org.uk/2009/Vol_3/paper4.pdf

[71] I use a lower best estimate correlation than normally found with equity markets these days. This is done to allow the aggregation theme in the text to come out more clearly. Also, 45% correlation, is low for a correlation between equity markets, but is more representative of correlation assumptions for risk factors other than equity. In this sense the example is more representative of what might be found in practice.

[72] Since the confidence interval used in the text is tighter than typically found in practice, the ensuing text later in the chapter shows less uncertainty than found in the industry. The text shows a lot of uncertainty. In practice, there is even more.

[73] To illustrate the potential cost associated with the time-0 stress methodology, suppose you have a liability of 100. Assets backing liabilities are 100. Suppose it is a liability from which we expect a profit of 1% (of liability) per year. This profit could be an asset management charge (AMC) net of expenses. It could be an expected risk profit, or similar type projection. Suppose the projected asset return and growth of liability are both 3%. Further, suppose, for whatever reason, that our capital requirement is shortfall versus liabilities when the assets backing liabilities are stressed 10%.

Instantaneous Stress Calculation:

Stressed Asset-backing-liability Value= $100 * (1 - 10\%) = 90$
Required Capital = $100 - 90 = 10$.

1-year horizon calculation:

Future Liability = $100 * (1.03) * (1 - 1\%) = 101.97$
Future value of Assets currently backing liabilities: $100 * (1.03) + 1\% * [100 * (1.03)] = 104.03$
Stressed Asset-backing-liability Value= $104.03 * (1 - 10\%) = 93.627$
Required capital = Liability Value - Asset Value = $101.97 - 93.627 = 8.343$.

In the regulations, there is no discounting back of the short fall. Therefore, the capital requirement of 8.343 is not discounted back to time zero.

The cost of using an instantaneous stress is, of course, $10 - 8.343 = 1.657$ in the above example.

Notice also, that the capital of 8.343 is expected (in a dynamic base case projection) to produce a return of 1. This represents a return on capital of about 12%. In Tip 49, the rule-of-thumb was that the cost is a year's return on capital, which is not true in the above example. The year's profit is expected to be 1, while the cost of a zero-stress implementation is 1.657. In this example, the cost is about 1.657 years worth of return on capital.

There are alternate calculations. In the above example, the 1% profit reduced the liability and increased the assets. Perhaps in some situations, this is not appropriate. Maybe only one of these changes is appropriate. In that case, the cost would be half as much, only 0.8285. This means the cost is less than one year's worth of profit. The exact cost of using the time-0 stress depends on the actual calculations used. The rule-of-thumb that the cost is a year of return on capital is just a rough estimate.

[74] For example, we could change the distribution used to have a mean of zero but maintain the 1-in-200 stress. In the text example, the return on sub-portfolio A has a mean of 10% and a 1-in-200 loss of -44%. We could replace this distribution with a normal distribution which has a mean (median) of zero but still has a -44% 1-in-200 level. This would "scrunch" the distribution a bit. The advantage of this is that this new distribution could be used as a time-0 shock. It would provide the same 1-in-200 year event as if we had done a horizon analysis, but would allow us to use systems that employ instantaneous shocks.

The deformation is conservative, providing only higher capital requirements (losses) for any interim quantile between the median and the 1-in-200 event. The use of killer scenarios, or the Curve of Constant Loss, would thus fulfil the Solvency II requirement of being at least as stringent as a 1-in-200 year event.

[75] I prefer to display uncertainty in a few ways.

1. Best estimate.
2. Highest and lowest effect of a single parameter (e.g. mean of x, standard deviation of y, etc.) change.
3. Highest and lowest effect of changing parameters for a single risk factor (e.g. all x parameters, all y parameters, etc.) change.
4. Effect of aggregation parameter changes. (In our example, this is the range of the correlation.)
5. Highest and lowest when all parameters are changed to extreme values simultaneously. All combinations are tried in order to find the extremes.

This form of staging addresses the issue raised in the text that perhaps not all parameters would deviate from our best estimate. This presentation shows the effect of different numbers of parameters changing at the same time.

In our example, we first change the parameters one at a time, fixing all others. The results of changing the single parameters of x and y one at a time have a lowest capital requirement of 214 and a highest of 420. The results are shown in the table below.

Parameters	x mean	x st.dev	x 1-in-200	Y Mean	Y st.dev	Y 1-in-200	Correlation	Required Capital
Best Estimate	10%	21%	-44%	6%	18%	-40%	45%	299
Vary x mean	7%	21%	-47%	6%	18%	-40%	45%	330
Vary x mean	15%	21%	-39%	6%	18%	-40%	45%	251
Vary x sdtev	10%	15%	-29%	6%	18%	-40%	45%	214
Vary x stdev	10%	29%	-65%	6%	18%	-40%	45%	420
All of x varies	15%	15%	-24%	6%	18%	-40%	45%	163
All of x varies	7%	29%	-68%	6%	18%	-40%	45%	449
Vary y mean	10%	21%	-44%	2%	18%	-44%	45%	327
Vary y mean	10%	21%	-44%	9%	18%	-37%	45%	280
Vary y stdev	10%	21%	-44%	6%	12%	-25%	45%	261
Vary y stdev	10%	21%	-44%	6%	26%	-61%	45%	363
All of y varies	10%	21%	-44%	9%	12%	-22%	45%	242
All of y varies	10%	21%	-44%	2%	26%	-65%	45%	390
Correlation	10%	21%	-44%	6%	18%	-40%	30%	273
Correlation	10%	21%	-44%	6%	18%	-40%	60%	359

[76] See the VaR of an elliptic distribution, see proposition 3.29 in "Quantitative Risk Management: Concepts, Techniques and tools," by Alexander j. McNeil, Rüdiger Frey and Paul Embrechts, Princeton University Press, 2005.

[77] One faulty method of determining a single killer scenario is to average all killer scenarios found. This is faulty since if your loss function is not linear, the average killer event may not have the same loss value, i.e. may not be a 1-in-200 event. This is because the Curve of Constant Loss is most likely not convex.

[78]   Portfolio mean is .6*E(x)+.4*E(y)=.6*10%+.4*(6%)=8.4%
         Portfolio variance is var(0.6x)+ var(0.4y) + 2(0.45) sqrt[var(0.6x) var(0.4y)] =(0.170953%)^2.

[79] By definition, an elliptical distribution on the vector x is of the form $f(x^T C x)$ where C is a correlation matrix. The class of elliptic distributions includes multivariate Normal and multivariate Student-t distributions, among others.

[80] The -44% and -40% returns are simple returns. In other words, the drop in the market value of the sub-portfolios is this amount. Stated mathematically, $e^{x_i} - 1 = -0.44$ and $e^{y_i} - 1 = -0.4$.

[81] As in the previous endnote, the means are the returns expressed in simple terms, i.e. mathematically, $E(e^{x_i} - 1) = +0.10$ and $E(e^{y_i} - 1) = +0.06$. These lead to means of the lognormal random variable of 9.53% and 5.83%, respectively.

[82] No simulation was used twice, i.e. there is no overlap of simulations for different estimates.

[83] For complex products, it may be necessary to make 100,000 or even 500,000 runs. Some applications in the author's experience have been recommended to have 1,000,000 simulations.

[84] The standalone loss for Risk factors 1 and 2 are 240 and 100, respectively, as in the case of the correlation matrix aggregation approach. Recall that we have synchronized the two examples to be identically calibrated.

[85] To estimate the Curve of Constant Loss, each point has been adjusted to account for the fact that its loss is not the aggregate loss. With risk factors f_1 and f_2, if $Loss(f_1, f_2) = L$ and the aggregate loss is L_{Agg}, then we estimate a point of the Curve of Constant Loss to be $\left(\frac{L_{Agg}}{L} f_1, \frac{L_{Agg}}{L} f_2\right)$. This is equivalent to a first order Taylor approximation of the loss function around the point (f_1, f_2). This should be reasonably accurate for points whose loss is close to the aggregate loss, as is the case for the points mentioned in the text. This approximation is not the cause of the Curve of Constant Loss appearing linear.

[86] I ran these 5,000 simulated losses through R. (R does not accept more than 5,000 points for some tests.) The best-fit Normal distribution failed the Anderson-Darling and Shapiro-Wilk tests for Normality. Furthermore, the Kolmogorov-Smirnov test for goodness of fit failed for all tested distributions: Normal, Student-t, Lognormal, Logistic, Gamma, Logistic, Cauchy and Weibull. This is not surprising. In practice, fitting any set of 10,000 points almost always fails these tests (unless the data is contrived) because the high N causes the test to demand a close fit to the tested distribution. It is difficult to match 10,000 points. All these tests were at the 99% level.

I emphasize the point made in the text: these tests failed because we placed too much reliance on the parameter estimates. When the parameter uncertainty is considered, we can fit a Normal distribution to the loss function.

[87] In fact, the Normal distribution breaks through the bounds slightly. The largest breakthrough in the example is for 0.18% that the Normal distribution is outside the bounds. It is also noteworthy that up to the 99.5% loss level (the killer scenario tail of the distribution), the Normal distribution does not break out of the bound at all.

We could use this largest break-though to devise a goodness-of-fit test by modifying the Kolmogorov-Smirnov test: the amount of that a potential distribution lies outside of a bound would replace the normal Kolmogorov-Smirnov statistic: $D_n = \sup_x |F_n(x) - F(x)|$. However, in such an approach, the true difficulty would be determining an appropriate n to use. We would always be able to make the test fail by increasing n sufficiently. However, it seems counter-intuitive that we should therefore conclude to reject a distribution in this manner. The boundary itself has uncertainty, depending on the certainty of the range of the parameter. Consideration should be made to compare the uncertainty of the parameter range with the results of a modified Kolmogorov-Smirnov test as described above.

[88] This initial Curve of Constant Loss is an unbiased estimator of the eventual one.

[89] To sample around the Curve of Constant Loss, we need to choose scenarios in a different manner from the shotgun Monte Carlo approach. Targeted Monte Carlo breaks the sampling into different rounds of sampling: an initial round, a second round and so forth. Between each round, the sampling distribution is adjusted to incorporate the results of the samplings already performed.

The initial stage of targeted Monte Carlo uses the exact same sampling methodology as standard (shotgun) Monte Carlo. The latter uses the underlying distribution of the risk factors to guide the selection of the sample scenarios. Like with standard Monte Carlo, with targeted Monte Carlo we order the initially sampled points according to loss. We identify the 1-in-200 loss. We find those points around the 1-in-200 loss and call them the initial Curve of Constant Loss.

For example, if for our initial sample, we were to sample 1,000 points, we would identify the 5th (or 6th) as the 1-in-200 event. We then might use the 3rd to 9th worst losses to estimate our initial Curve of Constant Loss. As mentioned in Endnote 85, we modify these points to determine our initial estimate of the Curve of Constant Loss. For this initial stage, the targeted Monte Carlo has been exactly like the shotgun Monte Carlo, except with fewer scenarios.

For the next round of sampling, we determine a method for sampling scenarios to test against our form-fitted loss function. For the second round and all subsequent rounds, we do not use the joint distribution of the risk factors to select scenarios to test. Instead, we develop a separate distribution to use for sampling. In mathematics,

$$g(f_1,...,f_N) = \text{the joint distribution of the risk factors } f_1,...,f_N.$$

$$h(f_1,...,f_N) = \text{the joint distribution used to sample the risk factors } f_1,...,f_N.$$

When using a sampling distribution not equal to the actual distribution, the calculation of the 1-in-200 loss must be adjusted. We weight the points to adjust for the sampling distribution. We would still order all the scenarios according to loss. Unlike Standard Monte Carlo, with targeted Monte Carlo each scenario does not have an identical weight. For each point sampled, we calculate a weight:

$$\text{Weight for sample point } (f_1,...,f_N) = g(f_1,...,f_N)/h(f_1,...,f_N).$$

When calculating the 1-in-200 loss, we do not count the sampled points equally. Instead, we find that point where 0.5% of the total weight (as calculated above) is for points with a greater loss, and 99.5% of the weight is associated with points with lower loss.

With this loss, as before, we can identify sampled scenarios for which the loss is close to that 1-in-200 loss. We modified these points close to the 1-in-200 loss, like before, so that each modified point has the same loss as the 1-in-200 loss. (See Endnote 85.) These modified points then form the basis to make a new Curve of Constant Loss. Let us call it Curve of Constant Loss-2. This ends the second portion of sampling. Notice that in this process, no new heavy lifts are performed.

We repeat the process. Using the Curve of Constant Loss-2, we produce a new sampling function $h_2(f_1,...,f_N)$. This is used to sample new scenarios points in a 3rd portion of sampling. While doing these samplings, we calculate the weights $g(f_1,...,f_N)/h_2(f_1,...,f_N)$. (Notice the subscript "2" on the h function.) The points are ordered by loss, and using the weights, the 1-in-200 loss is determined. We identify points from the 3rd sampling that are close to this 3rd estimate of the 1-in-200. We develop modified versions of the close points to all have the 1-in-200 loss. These modified points for the basis for developing a Curve of Constant Loss-3.

We repeat the process further until we feel comfortable that the Curve of Constant Loss-N is stable. This then becomes our final Curve of Constant Loss. All the points along this contour have the same loss, and this is the 1-in-200 loss, our capital requirement.

It must be emphasized that the periodic recalibration does not cause any new scenario testing nor does it require additional heavy lifts. We are still using the same number of scenarios.

This process answers the question, how many scenarios are necessary? Answer: as many as required to insure the Curve of Constant Loss is stable.

[90] The most recent runs of each module can be stored on a network. Each decision maker can rerun his own model to see the effect of her own decision. In this manner, she sees the effect of her actions and the effect on capital. This goes a long way to aligning everyone in the company to make capital efficient decisions.

[91] If there are N risk factors, then the number of correlations is $\binom{N}{2} = \frac{1}{2}N(N-1)$. The growth is quadratic.

[92] There is ambiguity as to the meaning of the correlation. Specifically, is the correlation between the risk factors ($f_1, f_2, \ldots f_N$) or between the related standalone losses ($L_1, L_2, \ldots L_N$)? In virtually all correlation matrix implementations, this distinction is blurred. Purists criticize the correlation matrix methodology, in part, because of this ambiguous use of the correlation parameters. However, as demonstrated in Chapter 6, the view taken by this author is that the huge uncertainty surrounding correlation is a much larger issue than the exact definition of the correlation we use. Whether you use correlation on risk factors or on losses, the uncertainty is large and material. This is true for all aggregation methods, not just the correlation matrix method.

Furthermore, this is not a limitation of the aggregation methodology per se. However, acknowledging this limitation of all methods allows us to concentrate on other aspects, those we can affect, namely speed of calculation.

This is the input-output correlation distinction. If the correlations are correlations of factors, then these are input correlations. If the correlations relate to losses, these are output correlations. The terminology arises from the loss function $f_i \xrightarrow{\;Loss\;Function\;} L_i$, which maps each standalone risk factor onto its ensuing loss. The factors are inputs to the loss function and the losses are outputs. Thus, taking correlations of the fs is referred to as input correlations, and of the L's is referred to as output correlations.

[93] For the operational risk example in the text, this is a composite binary lognormal distribution. We construct the loss function in the following way. The loss function is defined as:

$$Loss(x, y) = 1000 g_{60\%}(x) + 1000 g_{30\%}(y).$$

Here g_p is a composite distribution which has probability p of being zero and probability 1-p of being the log of a standard normal distribution. Mathematically, let $\Phi(x)$ be the cumulative distribution of the standard Normal. Then the cumulative distribution of g is given by:

$$g_p(z) = \begin{cases} 0 & \Phi(z) \leq p \\ \exp(\Phi^{-1}\left(\dfrac{\Phi(z)-p}{1-p}\right)) & else \end{cases}$$

A numeric approximation was made to find the 1-in-200 loss to be 13,325.

[94] There may be a chance to use another loss model, not linear, that does not require Monte Carlo. This might be worth some research, but a current general analytic method to use on functions other than linear is not known to the author.

[95] This "truing-up" of a killer scenario is often referred to as the "medium bang" approach.

[96] The diagram is from Page 90 of the QIS 5 Technical Specifications.
https://eiopa.europa.eu/fileadmin/tx_dam/files/consultations/QIS/QIS5/QIS5-technical_specifications_20100706.pdf

[97] CEIOPS' Advice for Level 2 Implementing Measures on Solvency II: SCR STANDARD FORMULA article 111(d) correlations gives the following correlation matrix:

	Market	Default	Life	Health	Non-Life
Market	1	.25	.25	.25	.25
Default	.25	1	.25	.25	.5
Life	.25	.25	1	.25	0
Health	.25	.25	.25	1	0
Non-Life	.25	.5	0	0	1

[98] It is possible to combine staged correlation matrices into big correlation matrix, but this is not unique. The final big correlation matrix depends on the SCR numbers. Furthermore, some big correlations matrices may not allow any staged versions, but in any case would depend on the SCR numbers used.

[99] When a big correlation approach is used, there invariably are "material" correlations and immaterial ones. Effort is made to get the material ones right. The immaterial ones are allowed to vary considerably. For example, to get a consistent correlation matrix, it must be positive semi-definite (PSD). A trial correlation matrix is often not PSD because the correlations were not made with consistent data sets, or may have been made with different methods, e.g. historical analysis for some and expert judgement for others. To make the correlation matrix PSD, the trial matrix must be adjusted, and typically, the immaterial correlations are allowed to vary more in order to keep the material ones less changed.

[100] For example, suppose we had 32 risk factors. The big correlation matrix approach would need $\binom{32}{2} = 496$ different correlation parameters. If however, we could create 4 modules each with 8 risk factors, then the number of correlation parameters would be $\binom{4}{2} = 6$ for the overall correlation matrix (4x4) and then $\binom{8}{2} = 28$ for each sub-modules matrix (8x8). In total, this is 6 + 4x28 = 118 correlations parameters. This is quite a savings from 496.

The reduction in correlations parameters is even greater if more stages are employed. For example, if as before there are 32 risk factors with 4 modules of 8 risk factors each. But suppose further that each of the 8 factors in each module could be further staged into 4 sub-modules of 2 parameters each. In this situation, the number of correlations parameters is $\binom{4}{2} = 6$ for the overall correlation matrix, then $\binom{4}{2} = 6$ for each of the correlation matrices of the 4 modules, and then 1 for each of the correlation matrices of the 2x2 sub-modules. In this case, the total number of correlation parameters is 6 + 4x6 + 16x1 = 46. This is a tremendous savings over the 496 correlation parameters necessary in a big correlation matrix. This example is the motivation for the statement in the text that savings in correlation parameters could be a factor of 10: 496 is more than 10 times 46.

[101] See Kjersti Aas, Claudia Czado, Arnoldo Frigessi, Henrik Bakken, "Pair-copula constructions of multiple dependence," Sonderforschungsbereich 386, Paper 487 (2006). http://epub.ub.uni-muenchen.de/. Or Doris Schirmacher, Ernesto Schirmacher, "Multivariate Dependence Modeling Using Pair-Copulas, (2008) SOA.

[102] A Monte Carlo aggregation component can always be below a correlation matrix component when staging is used. The reason for this is that the 99.5% loss that comes out of the Monte Carlo aggregation of

the lower model can be passed up to the model as a standalone result in the upper modules correlation matrix.

The reverse is true. A Monte Carlo module can be above a Correlation Matrix module.
Step 7 of the aggregation procedure produces the entire distribution of losses. As mentioned above, the Monte Carlo aggregation in the upper module has enough information.

Although many applications currently use the Correlation matrix approach, they do not calculate the entire distributions of losses. This is only because it is not perceived as necessary. Given the assumptions of the Correlation Matrix, it is straightforward to produce the full distribution of losses, even if your model does not currently do so. A typical correlation matrix set-up assumes linear losses and all risk are normal (or elliptical, like a Student-t distribution). From this, we can determine the distribution of losses.

[103] The astute reader will see that Tip 81 was motivated by the preceding example. It did not "prove" that linear losses could always be used. I do not believe it is true. Nor have I shown lots and lots of examples to illustrate that it is true. The reader would need to look at his or her own application to judge. It has simply been my experience that, when combined with the fitting tolerance associated with parameter uncertainty, linear loss functions can be justified far more often than the industry as a whole currently admits.

Our belief that we are more accurate than we are, specifically that our parameters are more certain than they actually are, may account for our tendency to look down on linear loss functions. We reject linear loss, as an industry, more often than we should.

Nonetheless, linear loss is not always acceptable.

[104] Monte Carlo routines require more simulations to explore more dimensions. A rough rule of thumb says that when you double the number of risk factors (dimensions) you double the required number of simulations. Conversely, if we halved the number of dimensions, we would halve the required number of simulations to get the same accuracy. If we run an 8th of our risk factors in an aggregation sub-module, that aggregation would generally require $1/8^{th}$ the number of runs. That is a reduction in run times. (Some say the reduction is better than this, but this is good enough for management presentations.)

[105] By the way, in general our understanding of interdependence is 2-dimensional. We speak of correlations between variables but this is only between 2 variables. A correlation matrix describes correlations between many variables, but only 2 at a time. If there is a dependence that extends beyond these relationships, your typical Monte Carlo method does not cover it. Our current thinking cannot really imagine it either.

For example, consider 3 risk factors, A, B and C. We can study/specify a correlation between each pair: A-B, A-C and B-C. This leads to 3 correlation assumptions. It could be that all the interdependence between these variables is captured by these 3 correlation estimates. However, maybe it is not fully captured. Maybe there is a relationship that A, B and C have that is over an above the sum of the 2-at-a-time correlations.

There is a name for this situation. If all interdependence between variables is captured by the 2-at-a-time correlations, then these variables are said to be *Conditionally Independent*. All models I have seen implicitly assume conditional independence. I could probably get away without bringing the term up, but in the interest of being complete, I say we should assume conditional independence.

Notice that I am not saying we should analyze higher orders of dependence. Quite the opposite. If it is not in your management thinking already, then it is likely not critical to your business. Virtually all of the models I have seen assume that all the (material) interdependence is captured by the correlations. Any relationship not captured by our 2-at-a-time correlation analysis does not affect our current models. In your Solvency II manual, note it as an expert judgement.

Even if we did work up a theory and notation to cover this, then it would likely be fraught with even more uncertainty than correlation itself.

Armed with conditional independence, we can divide and conquer the risk factors in a Monte Carlo aggregation the same way we did in the above correlation matrix approach.

[106] I calculated this as:

There are $\binom{25}{4}$ 4th-degree terms with no risk factor squared or cubed.

There are $25\binom{24}{2}$ 4th degree terms with one squared risk factor, and 2 other factors.

There are $\binom{25}{2}$ 4th degree terms with two squared risk factors.

There are $25\binom{24}{1}$ 4th-degree terms with one cubed risk factor and 1 other factor.

There are 25 4th degree terms with one fourth degree risk factor.

There are $\binom{25}{3}$ 3rd degree terms with no squared nor cubed risk factor.

There are 25x24 3rd degree terms with one squared risk factor and one other.

There are 25 cubed terms. There are 25 squared terms.

There are $\binom{25}{2}$ 2nd degree terms with no squared nor cubed risk factor.

There are 25 linear terms.

There is one constant term.

In total, this is 23,751. Eliminating the 4th degree terms gives 3,276 terms.

The set-up for these calculations is as follows:

In a Monte Carlo analysis, we piece together the loss functions for each individual standalone risk into one large loss function. Rather than a separate loss function for each risk driver, we define one loss function for all risk drivers:

Overall Loss($f_1, f_2, f_3, \ldots , f_N$)

We require this to match the standalone loss found in Step 2 in the text. Mathematically:

Overall Loss(Base case for all risk drivers, except f_i which is at 99.5% level)= L_i

We can also write this in the following way ("BC" means "Base Case"):

Overall Loss($BC_1, \ldots BC_{i-1}, f_i , BC_{i+1}, \ldots BC_N$) = L_i

We also require that the loss is zero in the base case:

190

Overall Loss(BC_1, ..., BC_N) = 0.

Given these known points, one for each standalone dimension N and one for the base case, we try to fit a formula. This requires fitting $N + 1$ points. A typical choice is a polynomial formula, and

Overall Loss(f_1, f_2, f_3, ... , f_N)= 1st, 2nd, 3rd and 4th degree terms in f_1, ... , f_N

The first thing to note is that we might try to fit cross terms. Instead of just limiting ourselves to the $N + 1$ points mentioned above, we could try combinations of different risk drivers, run those combinations in our specialized actuarial models (heavy lifts) to determine the combination loss. We then include these points when fitting the formula. This is an important aspect and I expound upon it below. Before that, let me mention a few other areas of interest in the fitting process.

The second thing to notice is that it is a choice to use a polynomial. In practice, other functions might be used. (See Endnote 107.)

The third thing to notice is that we can choose different degrees for the polynomial. For example, we could eliminate all 4th degree terms, limiting ourselves to 3rd degree polynomials.

The fourth thing to point out is that if we limit ourselves to only 1st degree terms, then we are assuming a linear model. This is what I meant earlier when I said the polynomial was more general than the linear. Linear is a special case of polynomial. As often quoted, the correlation matrix is a linear model, or essentially the same thing. The implication is that the correlation matrix assumptions are a special case of the Monte Carlo approach. There is a bit of prejudice here, since the implication is that the Monte Carlo approach is better since it is more generalized. The prejudice is that it is superior. Is this true? Are all those extra terms in the higher-degree polynomial really adding exponentially to the accuracy of our model?

[107] Consider for example trying to fit a general Black-Scholes option formula. The "risk factors" are stock price, strike (which can be a free parameter that we do not know), interest rate, dividend yield and volatility. Notice that I have fixed maturity, just to make a point. It is instructive to try fitting points for this formula. After all, the Black-Scholes option pricing formula is known. It makes a good test case to attempt to fit this 5-dimensional problem in order to see how good our fitting routines are. You may use as many points as you would like. Try it. It is almost impossible to get a good fit.

The reason can be seen. Consider the option premium versus stock price graph. Asymptotically, this is a horizontal line to the left and a 45°-line (Slope 1) to the right. No polynomial will do this. Any effort to fit a polynomial will inherit this square-peg-in-a-round-hole problem.

At the time of this writing, the UK Institute and Faculty of Actuaries has set up a group, the Curve Fitting Working Party, to explore the proper "bases" to use for formula fitting, asking the question: Instead of polynomials, what basic function should be used? This is a recognized problem. It is hard, and recognized as hard.

[108] The simplest correlation matrix approach may not run a heavy lift check of the final answer. The simplest correlation matrix approach (like the Standard Formula) simply uses the capital figure that comes out of the matrix. When a correlation matrix result is analyzed to determine a killer scenario, and that scenario is run through a heavy lift, this is called the "Medium Bang" approach.

[109] The Institute and Faculty of Actuaries in the UK is currently setting up a working party to see if other forms for formula fitting the loss function are possible to use and more generally what the issues are with using proxy models. This would be the basis for finding the Curve of Constant Loss, of course.

[110] Some implementations of Monte Carlo go out of their way to cluster points. A typical implementation would perform some runs to formula-fit the loss function. Then it would run 100,000 scenarios (or some other big number) using a formula fit. Then after identifying a single killer scenario, the model would perform many runs close to this killer scenario in an effort to determine the sensitivity of the result around the one killer scenario. The motivation for this clustering of runs is often for attribution purposes rather than understanding the formula fit well. Nonetheless, the use of precious Heavy lifts in the cluster manner may not be the most efficient application.

It is my view that spreading out the heavy lifts to understand the loss function better makes more sense.

[111] The price of a fixed bond under a zero-interest rate scenario is simply the sum of cash flows. This may not be an interesting business/economic valuation. (Well, in the current economy it is getting more relevant.) Still, this analytic calculation informs the Curve of Constant Loss, at least for bonds. This easy calculation would count as a heavy lift for our loss curve calibration, but it would not take tremendous resources to calculate. It would be a "cheap" heavy lift.

[112] As with the previous endnote, there is little economic information in this calculation, but it does help nail down a different portion of the loss function. Other extreme points might be: 0% or 100% mortality, inflation or currency movements, -100% price movement for example in shares, total lapse, and so forth.

[113] By using the methodology in the targeted Monte Carlo, we only need to estimate the Curve of Constant Loss, not the entire loss function.

[114] In fact, we would be passing a distribution for each equity and interest rate. The staging methodology emphasized that an entire distribution of losses is passed from a lower aggregation to a higher one. The situation describe in the text, in which aggregation over equity and interest rates is postponed to the upper stage, we must pass upward a distribution function, $ELoss$, of equity and interest rates.